killing

Religion

Cheryl Lacey Donovan

Giving Your Soul a Rise...One Page at a Time

PEACE IN THE STORM PUBLISHING, LLC.

P.O. Box 1152

Pocono Summit, PA 18346

Visit our Web site at

www.PeaceInTheStormPublishing.com

Killing

Religion

by Cheryl Lacey Donovan

Acknowledgements

This book is a clarion call to the body of Christ. It is my plea to the church to be about the Father's business. It is time out for church as usual and time in for the saving of lost souls.

I acknowledge the Lord and Savior of my life Jesus Christ and His awesome gift of salvation for me and all those who have sinned and are saved by grace.

I acknowledge His charge that we go and become fishers of men searching for the least, the last and the lost.

I acknowledge His call to go ye therefore and teach all nations in the name of the Father, the Son, and the Holy Ghost.

I acknowledge his awesome gift of unconditional love and I pledge to give it in the best way I know how to each of my brothers and sisters.

I acknowledge this book was difficult to write, but,

like Esther, if I remain completely silent at this time, relief and deliverance will come from someplace else. Yet, who knows whether I have come to the kingdom for such a time as this. Esther 4:14

Dedications

I dedicate this book to Ashley Haynes, Crystal Hypolite, Joycelyn Brown and the countless other people I have spoken to who are seeking God and having difficulty finding Him in the church.

Prologue

Let me be the first to say I love God and I love the church. It is just as much a part of me and who I am as my own skin. Nevertheless, I struggled for months with myself and with God as I pondered whether or not to even write this book. However, countless conversations with disillusioned people struggling with their spirituality and whether or not at this point, after way too many run ins with "Christians," they should even bother getting to know who Jesus is, made me realize I had no other choice than to put pen to paper and get the job done.

It goes without saying that this book reflects the

pain and sadness I feel because the church I love so dearly has abdicated its rightful position in the world. Killing Religion is a clarion call for the church to stand up and be everything God has called it to be. Now, having given my disclaimer, let's get started.

Amen! Hallelujah! Praise the Lord! He is good and He is worthy to be praised! There is nothing impossible for God! God can do anything but fail! Anyone even remotely familiar with the African American religious experience can attest to the fact that these words saturate the atmosphere of most services with a thick cloud of spirituality that is both tangible and heartfelt. Born into a ministerial family for whom these words were not only declared on Sunday, but every day of my life, I too am very familiar with these exclamations of praise and exaltation to an almighty God.

My upbringing in the church was a unique one to say the least. My mother and father were divorced when I was four years old and because of the custody arrangement made between the two of them, I found myself immersed in what could only be described as a cornucopia of religious experiences that ultimately shaped my view of the impact the church and religion has one's life.

My Dad, a prominent Baptist Pastor, made sure I had a thorough understanding of the Baptist experience; full of Baptist Training Unions, Sunday School, and the Baptist Sunday School Convention. While my mother, who had grown up African Methodist Episcopal AME, returned to her roots shortly after their divorce. Here I was exposed to a completely different set of viewpoints that focused primarily on methodical concepts and regimented responses. The Young People's Department, the Women's Missionary Society, and Lay leaders made up the foundation in this denomination. I was soon educated about the formation of the African Methodist church experience it was an offshoot of United Methodism born after Richard Allen, the founder of the AME movement was not allowed to worship freely in the all white United

Methodist Church. Years later when my mother moved to United Methodism, I found myself a member of one of the soon to be largest United Methodist Churches in the country. Primarily, African American in its makeup at the time, it was hard to believe that this denomination once shunned African Americans from its services. To this day, I still find myself dividing my time between each of these denominations. Throw in a brief stint in the Church of God in Christ, which by the way was formed by a group of Baptists in 1897, and the result is a very distinctive perspective on the religious Diaspora. I have seen several different denominational interpretations each uniquely born out of the dissatisfaction a group of people may have had with their church experience at the time. Each group's interpretation of scripture, their various focuses in their doctrines, and their strict belief that their way is the right way, the only way, is further embedded in their psyche because they are certain that only their denomination has been chosen "the one" by God; that it is their denomination with the "keys to the kingdom" so to speak. Their view is either based on where "Jesus built His church" or their idea that the "use of methods" and ecclesiastical authority to govern is the divine will of God. Others believe instruments have no place in worship because to use them would reject Christ as the head of the church in all things, cause division, make worship vain, and is just not a good work. I am sure David, the man after God's own heart, who by the way played the harp, would take issue with anyone who would say his worship was in vain. Still others believe wearing makeup is inappropriate. However, I have been hard pressed to find any real scriptural basis for any of these ideologies; only opinions and interpretations that unfortunately are taken out of context from the original writings.

Nonetheless, being a preacher's kid, my lessons began very early. I learned the proper vernacular and the proper protocol of who to thank when I got up to speak and how long my presentation should be. Not sure exactly who decides that a particular sermon or prayer should only be a certain number of minutes long. I always thought it best to allow the Holy Ghost to lead. But I digress.

I would be remiss if I didn't share the familiar rants of well meaning church mothers. "Don't walk behind the pulpit and don't touch the little table in the front with the words on it," they would say. I learned this before I could even read the words on the table. I am still trying to figure out what if anything that has to do with salvation or a personal relationship with God, but you'd best believe most of us have perfected that part of religion and wouldn't be caught dead doing either. I am pretty sure Jesus never had a pulpit or a little table. Neither did Paul, Peter, Timothy, or any of the other prolific leaders of the Bible. Yet, they seemed to do just fine at bringing people into the knowledge of God. They seemed to know exactly how to be fishers of men without the props. I believe it was Peter who through the power of the Holy Spirit converted 3000. I have not yet figured out how these practices are applicable to my life or how they help me or anyone else love God or their neighbor any better. Nevertheless they both have become as engrained in our religious services as the sermon.

I guess I should not be surprised that I have come to this place in my life. I clearly remember several occasions as a child when I would go to my Father's closet, pull out one of his neck ties and begin a discourse mimicking what I had seen earlier that Sunday; perhaps a prelude to what was to come. However, for several years, I struggled with religion. Why, because as a woman called by God to deliver the good news of the gospel there was, and still are, some religious observers who would question the will of God for my life. Even though they say they believe God is powerful enough to speak the entire world into existence, there are still some, who when faced with the reality of a female preacher, would now say there is nothing impossible for God, except, His ability to call a woman to deliver the Word. Even though most of them are no doubt familiar with the passage of scripture in which God made a donkey talk, "And the LORD opened the mouth of the ass, and she said unto Balaam, What have I done unto thee, that thou hast smitten me these three times? And Balaam said unto the ass, because thou hast mocked me: I would there were a sword in mine hand, for now would I kill thee. And the ass said unto Balaam, Am not I thine ass, upon which thou hast ridden ever since I was thine unto this day? was I ever wont to do so unto thee? And he said, Nay. " Numbers 22:28-30 As well as the scripture where He declares He could have made the rocks cry out, "And he answered and said unto them, I tell you that, if these should hold their peace, the stones would immediately cry out. " Luke 19:40. Sadly, the spirit of religion contin-ues to imprison those who believe our sovereign God would not call me, a woman, to spread the good news. For their defense they use words spoken by Paul, an apostle of God who was speaking, not in specifics, but in generalities to a group of churches in Corinth who had strayed from the teachings Paul had given them originally. How do I know this? I was taking ministry classes and found myself in need of materials that would help me with Greek and Hebrew translations. So, who did I ask; my father who had been in ministry over forty years at the time. He loaned me one of his King James Bibles with lexicons in back. I still use it.

As all good preachers do, he had several pages paper clipped together with a note that held a sermon title from one of his previous messages. On the very next page was the scripture where Paul talks about women being silent in the church. Because this was a King James study Bible, it had notes on the bottom of every page that gave explanations for various scriptures. Imagine my surprise when this KJV version of the Bible said that this text was not in relation to women preachers. In fact, it went on to expound upon the fact that this statement was not even being made by God Himself. Duh! Since that moment, I have not looked back.

That being said, it should be made clear that I, like most Christians, have been very sincere in my desires to please God and do the right thing. I am a good wife, good mother, and a good Christian, but there has been something missing. I have had a blessed life. Not an easy one, but a blessed one. My Savior has been with me every step of the way since I accepted Him at the age of sixteen. There has never been a moment in my life since that time that I felt alone. Even in my darkest hours, I've cried out to Him for deliverance and He has always answered. Not always when I wanted, or in the way I wanted, but always an answer; the best one for me. It is this personal relationship I have with Him that has kept me. Not the pulpiteer, not the choir, not the religious tradition, not the denomination, but a personal one on one relationship with the one who created me. Because of this relationship I am not only a daughter of God, but I have been given a responsibility in my Father's vineyard; one that I do not take lightly, one that I contemplated for far too long because of the religious opposition to the charge I was given.

I have always been aware that the religious environment I grew up in is about doing, acting, performing, working, being effective, knowing the rules, and doing the right things; the emphasis on productivity, effectiveness and practicality instead of equipping the saints with knowledge and understanding and building up the body of Christ. It was about being a good follower and doing the work of the church no questions asked. At its root, all of this is good, but is it really God?

It goes without saying, working, performing, acting, and doing have their respective places in our Christian walk because God wants us to be agents of transformation in this broken world. He wants us to be diligent. He wants us to be disciplined. But, should not there be something more; something in addition to blind alle-

giance to a particular denomination or a particular religious leader, something that sustains us when the denomination or the leader succumbs to their humanness
and makes a mistake or misses the mark?

The truth of the matter is there are many people
who have lived and died never having professed Christ.
No one can dispute the evidence which indicates they
were just as sincere in their beliefs as I am in mine. So,
it's obvious that sincerity is just not enough. Neither is
simply following the majority because it seems like the
right thing to do. You see, an intellectual knowledge of
who God is may be fine, but an experiential knowledge is
so much better. Your experience with God should reflect
pure joy not only on the inside but on the outside. Being
saved does not mean being sinless but it does mean being covered by the blood of the Lamb. It means you may
not see the good in me, but God does because He looks
at me through the eyes of mercy and grace. When you
have this experiential knowledge, this personal relation-

ship, it carries you through the ups and downs of life. It keeps you focused on the end result which is victory. Not because of whom you are, but because of whom He is. It transcends the condemnation and the judgment of denomination, religious culture, and manmade systemization and governance. It takes you to a place of redemption, restoration, and wholeness that no man can take away. This is what I have come to know. This is relationship not religion. It has allowed me to walk freely an unapologetically in my calling.

This freedom is the freedom God has always desired His people to feel; an intimate relationship between Him and His people; the kind of relationship that finds us discerning His truth in our inner most being, in our soul. It is in this place that I have truly experienced God and Christianity. Intellectually pursuing an understanding of who He is only leads to more dysfunction in the body as man seeks to explain the unexplainable by interpreting the Word based on limited knowledge and understanding.

When the secret places of our lives have been un-covered and the façade we have so craftily erected has been chipped away a soul connection takes place. This is where God seeks to commune with us; the meeting place between body and spirit. This is where the fight begins; our emotions, feelings, and thoughts; our soul; the part of us we can't see, mixed with what we can see.

It's the totality of who we are; the truest place in us. The battle of a lifetime is fought over our souls. Our souls are lively, passionate, colorful, deep and beauti-ful. When souls are truly fed, we are brought to life in a way that is inexplicable. In turn, we give life to others. When we dishonor our souls, we eventually choke and die. This is why it is so important to feed our souls truth; not watered down theory or misguided interpretation and opinions, but the truth of God's Word as He and He alone reveals it to us as we mature spiritually in Him.

The weariness, the loneliness, the emptiness that

many of us feel comes from living in a world that largely ignores the deep needs of our souls and far too often when we turn to the body of Christ the need is diminished, marginalized, and all too frequently dismissed altogether. We are inundated with Scripture, but rarely told how to apply them to our lives or our situations. Even worse, the more severe the circumstance, the further under the rug it goes. Our souls are weary and too many of our churches are filled with people who have been in church all their lives, but because of selective memory they can't remember a time when they were lost. Therefore, they are useless to the new believer because their testimony remains hidden in the closet they've built to protect their title.

Religion as we know it, as I have grown to know it, is empty; full of wonderful words and kind gestures, whoops and hollers, rules and regulations, but nothing that creates a meaningful transformation, a true conversion of the soul that is long lasting and sustaining;

nothing that renders real deliverance and freedom from bondage. There is no place in religion to rest, to simply be in God's presence. Time constraints, orders of service, and rituals have replaced worship, pure and simple. There is really nothing about many of the religious ideas we have created that awakens, touches, fills, or satisfies desires for intimacy, for connection. Nothing that screams there is a place for refuge, a place for unconditional love, a place for restoration. This is why you see the same people at the altar Sunday after Sunday seeking the same deliverance from the same issues; the reason why the occurrences of miracles, signs, and wonders are so scarce. Yet, scripture is clear that the greatest commandment from God is love, and in order to have that love, one must create relationship and intimacy.

Let's look at Jesus and His various encounters and how He continuously reflected love while here on earth. Luke 10: 38-42 tells us about Mary and Martha. Mary's primary goal was simply to have a relationship with Jesus. She was all about gleaning from Him, learning from Him, identifying with Him.

Martha, on the other hand, was all about works. In fact, she was upset that Mary was sitting at the feet of Jesus rather than helping her to do the work. She mumbled and complained, and even asked Jesus to rebuke Mary and to send her to help with the busyness of the day. How appropriate for us even now. In the church the circumstances in our lives call us to be Marathas'. We busy ourselves doing good things. We shine in the hospitality ministry. We are president of the choir. We thrive as a leader in the missionary society. We want to serve, to give, to make a difference. We have our programs and our auxiliaries, our boards and our meetings. Yes, There is a lot of busy work going on in the church. The question remains however, is it God's business. How many souls are being saved while you are voting on who will be the next officer? How many are being brought to

Christ as you create the budget for the following year? Whose life is being changed while you create new rules and regulations to govern the body and keep them in line with your agenda? If Jesus came back today would any of this matter to Him? Would He say, "Good job keeping the doors of the edifice open." Or would He be more concerned about the lives you helped transform.

Then there is the woman with the issue of blood. She was ostracized, shunned, pushed to the side. However, when she touched Jesus with her faith He immediately knew it. The disciples still wanted to keep her in obscurity but Jesus wanted to know who it was that had so much faith.

Today we shun, ostracize, talk about, and push away those with issues in our churches. Instead of embracing them, praying for them, and offering them hope in a risen savior, we immediately cast stones. We condemn instead of uplift. Yet, in the example of Jesus we see that because of His undying love He is saying who has touched me with their faith. Who has sought me out in spite of the difficulty they have faced maneuvering through the crowd of people? Sometimes, like this woman, we are so bogged down that we don't think we can make it to Jesus. But there is a time to admit how desperately we need Jesus to comfort us, touch us, love us. Mary realized that, so she sat down and let Him minister to her. The woman with the issue of blood realized this and she pressed her way in spite of her situation.

The greatest challenge of our lives is learning to let God love us. I believe God is trying to embrace us, heal us, and transform us with love constantly; but religion clouds the pathway with its double minded rhetoric that often says do as I say and not as I do. Confused, too many of us don't know how to receive God's love because it would require us to let our guard down, to unmask ourselves and be transparent. We are afraid people will know that we have not always been the self righteous saints we are now, so we move from birth to

27

death with our most fundamental need unmet: circum-spectly, as the church, full of people with this unmet need, we are unable to extend that love to others in a way that is non-judgmental and non- condemning.

Religion and Christianity have become just a good philosophy to live by; there is value in its teachings, but far too often, there is nothing in it to truly touch our souls. Nevertheless, we claim that Christianity is about a relationship with a living person.

If relationship is where the true spiritual life begins, then we must all listen to God's voice. The voice of love, a voice that says, "Let me love you. " In so doing, that love will be translated into meaningful relationships that bring about true conversion and a lifelong journey of holiness.

INTRODUCTION

..."having a form of Godliness, but denying the power thereof; from such turn away. For of this sort are they which creep into houses, and lead captive silly women laden with sins, led away with divers lusts Ever learning, and never able to come to the knowledge of the truth. 2 Timothy 3:5-7"

One of the things I hear most often when speaking to people who are fed up with church is how hypocritical the people in the church really are. It's really not that these people are non-believers necessarily it's just that they are put off by the "do as I say not as I do" mentality of many in the church today. They don't see or feel the love, the compassion, the humility of Christ in those professing to be his followers. All they experience is the condescending half hearted attempt at bringing them into the fold through words they don't understand and ideas that are unfamiliar. This text conceptualizes what potential new believers and disappointed old ones vying with religiosity identify as there reason for not wanting to identify with religion. Here, Paul is not speaking of some godless group of individuals who know nothing about Christianity. He is speaking directly to believers. Not just the benchwarmers either. Paul is speaking to those with positions; the ones who create the Bible studies and lead the Sunday school lessons; the ones who have perfected the fine art of acknowledging and keeping the law yet somehow neglect to tell the truth in love instead of with contempt. He is talking to the Bible toting, scripture quoting individuals of his time and he is saying to them your religion is empty. You are lovers of yourselves, lovers of money, unthankful, despisers of

God, haughty, loving pleasure more than God, - sound familiar? Well, while these words were actually written by Paul thousands of years ago, they could easily have been written yesterday. Why, because messages strewn across pulpits Sunday after Sunday have become little more than self-help lessons, anemic in their ability to transfuse power into the souls of the people. These souls have been left empty, hungry for more, and un-nourished because what they really seek is the bread of life, the truth of God's Word.

It would be easy for us to pass judgment on un-believers we know that fit the description of what Paul is speaking of. But, on the contrary, Paul is admonish-ing us as believers to be introspective; to do some soul searching. He wants us to ask ourselves "God could this be me? Could I be holding on to what I think is godli-ness, yet, I've denied the power to transform me from the inside out?"

These may indeed be bad times but the church is

not fading because of bad times; it is becoming extinct because of bad people. Their ways may seem right to them but their customs, precepts, and dictums represent the perfect definition of "religion" - an organized system of beliefs, ceremonies and rules, devotion to religious faith or observance, an institutionalized system of attitudes, beliefs, and practices. Nowhere in this definition do we find any mention of God and the need for knowing who He truly is and how He wants to transform our lives for the better.

Yes, religion has meandered through the pathway of time finally coming to stop in a place where it tells us what we want to hear rather than what we need to hear. A place where its leaders and inhabitants are more concerned about their edicts, standardization and governance than the truth of the gospel; a gospel that leads to Jesus instead of the immaculately adorned four walled edifices with stained glass windows and ornate chandeliers that we perceive to be the "church" and the well rehearsed, programmed orators we have come to know as the "preachers. "

The messages delivered in this place where religion lives neglect to tell us the Spirit of God lives within each of us and that we are the manifestation of God's kingdom here on earth. Instead we are indoctrinated to follow the leader playing a dangerous game of Simon Says that in some cases leads away from the path of righteousness and directly, discreetly, and indiscriminately into the gates of hell. Many have been trained to believe more in the messenger than in the message. Because of this belief which hinges upon human frailties and faults, many have left the "church" when the "shepherd" has engaged in less than holy behaviors. The fallout from such is usually more than many believers, especially new ones, can bear.

Religion and the "church" have become corrupted by mindsets and principles that have compromised our understanding of true Kingdom living in these last days.

Instead of being in preparation for the coming of the Bridegroom like the 5 wise virgins, we are more like the five foolish virgins who because of their lack of intimate relationship with God depleted their lamps of oil. We are conformed to the world; doing things like the world does. We've become lovers of ourselves, making our own will the center of our lives. It is no longer "thy will be done" but "my will be done. " Along the way both divine and human relationships have been obliterated resulting in a lack of obedience to God and no room for charity to men. In fact, these days all you have to do is turn on the television and you will hear of one scandal after another that deals with the downfall of prominent pastors or ministries that have fallen short. I often wonder where the praying saints were as these pastors and ministries were being inundated by the enemy. Is it not our obligation, even our responsibility, to go to the aid of our brothers and sisters when they have fallen? Aren't we to cast out demons and pray for one another? Where are the spirits of forgiveness and long suffering?

Aren't we all too eager, just as the world, to slander the brethren, malign their names, and throw them under the proverbial bus? Is this truly what the "church" is called to do? Religion says it is.

Our rules say if you do "XYZ" then we can put you out of the church or take back our credentials and put you out. Really, throw you out of the church? Well, maybe "your" church. I am glad God does not have the same philosophy. If He did I am sure my brothers Moses and Paul who were both murderers would be goners. Furthermore, what about Noah the alcoholic? And who could forget David the adulterous man after God's own heart that had his best friend killed because he wanted to sleep with his wife Bathsheba? Religious doctrines of our day would have each of these men tried in the public eye and excommunicated because of their transgressions. There would be no Red Sea deliverance, no road to Damascus, and no new beginning for mankind because of the Ark. Yet, each of these men was an important building block in God's blueprint, his architectural design, his master plan for the building of His church.

We are blinded by our self righteous pious attitudes. This spiritual blindness hides the truth of God because we find what we read in Scripture hard to accept; therefore we interpret the Word to meet our own selfish needs and desires. Self-delusional and self centered in our actions, religion's stronghold on the church has caused it to fail in completing its purpose in the world.

We have detoured tremendously from Pentecost which was the day when the Holy Ghost did something that had never been seen before. On that day lives were noticeably transformed in the upper room. More than 3000 were convicted, convinced, and converted; ushering in a new era and new entity know as the church. This was a new dispensation like none other seen before. However, having begun in this blaze of power, glory, and authority today's church unfortunately finds itself being blinded by the god of this world who has taken the spirit of religion and used it to his advantage. Isaiah compares this blindness to a "veil spread over all nations. " Isaiah 25:7 Religion has caused the church to decline into an empty, lifeless, ritualistic practice that co-exists with the world instead of transforming the world. Our need to put ourselves rather than others first has led to a dysfunction in the family of believers. This dysfunction causes some in the body to believe the church belongs to them rather than God. It causes others to believe they can give and take the right to preach at their discretion forgetting all the while that "whom He did predestinate, them he also called, and whom He called, them he also justified, and whom He justified, them He also glorified. Romans 8:30 "But these are the last days of the church ushered in on the Day of Pentecost. God is about to do a new thing as He begins His healing of the spiritual blindness that plagues His church by casting out the spirit of religion that holds the church in captivity.

One must not forget the church's true role has always been to be called out of the world so that through the power of the Holy Ghost we would reignite a revival. To the contrary it has become clear that the devil also goes to church dressed up in his robe of religion. Arguably he probably spends more time at church than he does anywhere else because he knows if he can cause discord among the brethren he can put a stop to the fulfilling of our role as the salt of the earth. But it is extremely difficult for those with strong religious convictions to relinquish what they have already learned in error. Subsequently, the enemy and his religion is succeeding in draining the strength and power out of the body of Christ by enforcing philosophies that have little if anything to do with salvation. Our influence is slowly slipping away while we focus most of our time on our prohibitions, laws, and rehearsed practices. Spiritual power is being replaced and transformed into a mere shadow of itself through the smoke screen of pomp and circumstance we have immersed ourselves in through ceremonial chanting and reciting on cue. Christianity and the church is not suppose to be about keeping ordinances and following ritualistic edicts sent down by an ecclesiastical headquarters. It is suppose to be about the leading of the Spirit of God. "For as many as are led by the spirit of God they are the sons of God. " Romans 8:14. We have to be careful not to miss the mark. We must strive to be led by the Spirit and not by a schedule.

Formalism created an outward appearance of godliness but not an inward conviction of holiness even in the days of Jesus. This was the problem of the Jewish people in the first century. "But their minds were blinded: for until this day remaineth the same veil untaken away in the reading of the Old Testament; which veil is done away in Christ. But even unto this day, when Moses is read, the veil is upon their heart. Nevertheless when it shall turn to the Lord, the veil shall be taken away. " 2 Corinthians 3:14-16. They thought they understood Scripture. They thought they were living by Scripture. All the same, they were deceived by their own preconceived notions; their own way that seemed right to them. The problem is this meant everything they did was about pleasing people and every decision they made was about what others would say or do. It was based on law and not on love. It was for men and not for God. It pleased their flesh but not their Spirit. It was all about action and not unction.

We too suffer from the spirit of religion. In other words we have lots of programs but we have no power. We are good at bake sales, clubs, and projects but where is the power of God? We know when to recite certain scriptures and sing certain songs but what about the Holy Spirit? We are doing a lot of good things but what about the God things? Who is being saved in our annual meetings, convocations, and conventions? Who is being delivered?

Maneuvering through the fog of self righteousness, sanctifying sin has regrettably become our light in the midst of the haze. We bring our sin to church and reclassify it as "being human. " Moreover, we declare it as ignorance so that we can better tolerate it. But even the world knows ignorance of the law does not excuse you from keeping the law. To make matters worse we live sinful lives under the cover of membership and even leadership. Because of religion church has become just another club that will help us feel good about ourselves. We are out of control. The same offenses that are in the world; sex, drugs, alcohol and others have infiltrated not only the pews but the pulpit. And so as not to be confused, the law of sowing and reaping applies both for the good and the bad. If you are sowing hell in the pulpit you will reap hell in the pews. If you sow discord in the pulpit you will reap the same in the pews. We suffer from a "salad bar" religion picking and choosing what we want; faith sprinkled with a little favor and topped with prosperity or perhaps a drizzle of victory with no real battle. This mentality causes the body of Christ to suffer in ways that reverberate all the way to heaven. We see another church growing or a particular preacher getting invitations to preach around the country and we become envious wondering how it could be that we are not getting the same type of invitations. After all we preach better than them, don't we? Surely our musical repertoire warrants a call or two. And let's not forget the amount of study and educational commitment we put into this. Because of these self indulgent reactions, we begin to incorporate what that church, pastor or minister is doing in their ministry into our routine instead of walking in the plans God has for our lives. We begin to change our sound and we begin to change our actions trying to be more like them. We begin practicing our whoop and perfecting our praise dance, wrongfully believing that if we start using this discourse or that form of delivery, then we will begin to prosper like them. We are literally trying to keep up with the spiritual Jones's because we have convinced ourselves that there is some quick fix, some easy way, and some magical approach to spiritual success. We want 2000 members, a 500 voice choir, a big new church with stained glass windows and fiberglass pulpit. We want a praise dance team, two services and an entourage to follow us wherever we go but what we need to do is operate in the measure of grace God has given us. With a spirit of excellence working in the gifts and talents endowed to us by God we can be assured that God will honor our obedience because when operating in our proper position we need only to sit back and watch what God will do. Realistically you don't know what type of hell that church or those church leaders had to go through to get to where they are. You see their glory but you don't know their story. Stop trying to be like everyone else and start trying to be more like Christ because the lusts of the flesh are leading us away from our first love; Christ.

The rulers of darkness of this world know exactly what to say and how to say it. But the things they lead us to never reveal the truth. We hear sermon after sermon yet, we are never truly delivered and set free. We never really come into the true knowledge of God and who

He is. We only "hear" the Word; we don't study it or meditate on it. Therefore, it is no surprise that we never "do" or practice the Word. Even in the day of "new age" power the body of Christ must be hyper vigilant and not seduced by religion and those masquerading as angels of light. Jesus is not coming back for a defeated church.

He is coming back for one that has victory. Our job is to put ourselves into position by identifying ways to establish the kingdom in our lives and the lives of others. Doing this robs the enemy and all his demons of their power over us.

It is our God given right to influence the world for Christ. We are the Kingdom of God here on earth. We must take our rightful place and use our authority to take dominion. Every word of Scripture, every Bible study, and every act of God to this point has been and should be about the restoration of the Kingdom.

Understanding our royal priesthood lineage is a key component to gaining access to everything we need.

Scripture reminds us Jesus is King of Kings and Lord of Lords. Therefore it is implied we are kings and lords destined to live the abundant life Jesus came died and rose again for us to live.

Killing Religion is an insightful look into where the church is now and where it needs to be in the end times. It examines the fruits that Jesus said should identify the church as well as the fruits borne by those who preach and follow the gospel of self. It is a wakeup call for those who profess to be believers. In the face of the current condition of the church and religions place in it, we can expect that many will vilify, even denounce, those who speak against some of its modern day trappings. Killing Religion admonishes us not to succumb to the social persecution that will inevitably come as we diligently seek to follow Christ. Even as evil men and impostors grow worse and worse, Killing Religion encourages us to seek to live lives reflective of the God that dwells inside us. Killing Religion cautions us to turn away from our dead religion and to repent from our dead works because God is not moved by the performance of religious deeds if our heart isn't right, if we are not engaged with the Spirit.

Killing Religion will help you focus on identifying your assignment rather than your position because when we operate in the spirit of assignment we understand the purpose God has for our life and we don't worry about trying to sound like or act like someone else. Operating in what God has called us to, makes us keenly aware His grace is sufficient. However, when we get out of our lane we open ourselves up to the attack of the enemy and we become discouraged when things are not going smoothly for us like they are for someone else. Therefore, envy, strife, and malice grab hold of our minds because we are out of grace. Allow Killing Religion to help you unlock the kingdom of God in your life. Discover how to tap into the power of the kingdom that is within you so that you no longer just do church you become the church.

THE ORIGINAL CHURCH

"I will build my church; and the gates of hell shall not prevail against it. " Matthew 16:18

While many mainstream Christian denominations of our time would like to hold the coveted position of being the church "God intended," the reality of the situation is that most of them fall short. Why because they have succumbed to their own selfish ambition, their own reality of "religion" and its place in the Kingdom of God. Entitlement and pride has become the flavor of the day leaving much to be desired when it comes to compassion, forgiveness, and love; all of which are attributes of what God really desires of His church. "Church hurt" has become a relevant term describing the sentiment felt by those, no less children of the most high than anyone else, relegated to infancy by "the righteous" because they have trespassed some rule or regulation, dressed inappropriately, or perhaps have simply sat in the favorite pew of the spiritual elite.

Therefore, in order for a book of this kind to be received in the manner in which it was intended, it is necessary to begin at the beginning; to look at the scriptural basis of the early church, the one Jesus created. An examination of the characteristics of this church will allow us to see with open eyes how far we have digressed due to our non-biblical mores, philosophical conclusions and cultural beliefs. As we look at the original church we will focus on the church in Jerusalem which had the direct supervision of the Lord's apostles for several years.

The Jerusalem church in the New Testament spans

a period of twenty to thirty years. The church was established in 30 A. D. , Gentiles entered the church in 40 A. D. , the council on circumcision in Jerusalem was held in 50 A. D. , and Paul was assaulted and imprisoned in Jerusalem in 58 A. D.

It is clear the church began during the biblical festival of Pentecost 50 days after Jesus' resurrection from the dead. Prior to Pentecost the church is spoken of as being in the future. "And I say also unto thee, That thou art Peter, and upon this rock I will build my church; and the gates of hell shall not prevail against it. " Matthew 16:18.

After Pentecost it is spoken of as being in the city of Jerusalem. "And when the day of Pentecost was fully come, they were all with one accord in one place. And suddenly there came a sound from heaven as of a rushing mighty wind, and it filled all the house where they were sitting. And there appeared unto them cloven tongues like as of fire, and it sat upon each of them.

And they were all filled with the Holy Ghost, and began to speak with other tongues, as the Spirit gave them utterance. And there were dwelling at Jerusalem Jews, devout men, out of every nation under heaven. " Acts 2. Obviously this is the place where the church of Christ began. It was in Jerusalem that the Holy Spirit came upon the apostles, the gospel was preached, and 3000 were baptized into the body of Christ.

Before the coming of the Holy Spirit on the Day of Pentecost Jesus' apostles were ordinary people much like you and I. Yet, after Pentecost they became formidable leaders in the Body of Christ. It was this combination of the Holy Spirit and the people that created the church.

The four Gospels—Matthew, Mark, Luke and John—talk about each of the apostles and their lifestyles before they came into contact with Jesus. There are no references that any of the disciples were influential or well educated. In fact, religious leaders of the day would probably have seen them as unlearned and beneath them. "Now when they saw the boldness of Peter and John, and perceived that they were unlearned and ignorant men, they marveled; and they took knowledge of them, that they had been with Jesus. "Acts 4:13.

Matthew was a tax collector, a member of one of the despised professions of his day. "And as Jesus passed forth from thence, he saw a man, named Matthew, sitting at the receipt of custom: and he saith unto him, Follow me. And he arose, and followed him. " Matthew 9:9. Peter, his brother Andrew, and two other brothers, James and John, were partners in a modest fishing enterprise. "And Jesus, walking by the sea of Galilee, saw two brethren, Simon called Peter, and Andrew his brother, casting a net into the sea: for they were fishers. And he saith unto them, Follow me, and I will make you fishers of men. And they straightway left their nets, and followed him. And going on from thence, he saw other two brethren, James the son of Zebedee, and John his brother, in a ship with Zebedee their father, mending their nets; and he called them. And they immediately left the ship and their father, and followed him. " Matthew 4:18-22 Along with Philip, they lived in the town of Bethsaida in the northern province of Galilee. "Now Philip was of Bethsaida, the city of Andrew and Peter. " John 1:44. The one thing that made them special was that they were called by Jesus to become His disciples, students and followers.

In Scripture, we find Jesus consistently rebuking the apostles for being still controlled by their carnal natures. Even though they were His students, even though they had seen Him do all kinds of miracles, signs, and wonders, they still lacked enough faith to fully walk in their callings. In fact, their unbelief stunted their spiritual growth. One example is when Jesus sternly chastised James and John for their attitude toward some who had rejected Jesus: "But they [the Samaritans] did not receive Him . . . And when His disciples James and John saw this, they said, 'Lord, do You want us to command fire to come down from heaven and consume them, just as Elijah did?' But He turned and rebuked them, and said, 'You do not know what manner of spirit you are of. For the Son of Man did not come to destroy men's lives but to save them' Luke 9:53-57. Even though he didn't exhibit much of it in this text, John would later become known as "the apostle of love. "

Selfish at their core, we see another example of the carnality of the apostles when James and John tried to trick Jesus into awarding them the two most prominent positions in His Kingdom. "And James and John, the sons of Zebedee, come unto him, saying, Master, we would that thou shouldest do for us whatsoever we shall desire. And he said unto them, What would ye that I should do for you? They said unto him, Grant unto us that we may sit, one on thy right hand, and the other on thy left hand, in thy glory. " Mark 10:35-37.

Lastly, After Jesus was resurrected; He appeared to

.

His gathered disciples, except for Thomas, who was not present. Upon hearing about this, Thomas was so skeptical that he commented, "Unless I see in His hands the print of the nails, and put my finger into the print of the nails, and put my hand into His side, I will not believe" John 20:25. Jesus later appeared and provided Thomas with the precise proof he requested verses 26-29. Later still, Peter and six of the other apostles decided it was time to resume their former work as fishermen. "There were together Simon Peter, and Thomas called Didymus, and Nathanael of Cana in Galilee, and the sons of Zebedee, and two other of his disciples. Simon Peter saith unto them, I go fishing. They say unto him, we also go with thee. They went forth, and entered into a ship immediately; and that night they caught nothing. " John 21:2-3. They had actually met with the risen Christ, but their limited perspective still blinded them to the significance of Jesus' sayings and what He intended for them to do. That same blindness is a part of all human beings until God opens their understanding to see what He really says in His Word.

Chosen by Jesus, these men were handpicked to carry His gospel to any and everyone who would listen. However, having not yet received the power of the Holy Spirit they were powerless; devoid of the ability to fulfill their own destinies and faithfully serve their Savior. Their own strength was not enough to save them or anyone else. We too would do well to understand that it is not by our own power that we are saved. It is not by our own power that we are elevated to leadership and positions of stature. Instead it is the power of the Holy Spirit that works on the inside of us that leads us and guides us into the will of God for our lives. However, far too often we read our own press and fall into the trap of our own narcissism and conceit. It becomes about what we've done for the church. How we've succeeded in our endeavors and how we have been elevated because of our own works.

The disciples asked, "Who then can be saved?" Jesus answered: "With men this is impossible, but with God all things are possible" Matthew 19:25-26. Through the indwelling of the Holy Spirit, Jesus Christ and God the Father can actively participate in the lives of every Christian to strengthen and inspire them in their obedience and service to God.

On the day of Pentecost having received the Holy Ghost, this spiritually transformed body of believers, changed instantly by the Spirit of God, practiced separation from the world, unconditional love, and childlike obedience to the teachings of Jesus Christ. These characteristics were what separated the disciples and early Christians from the rest of the world. The transformation of the people of God through His Spirit was and still is a transformation of the heart, the innermost being. Because of this transformation believers gained an obedient spirit, instead of hard-heartedness and hostility to God's laws. God was working in them; He dwelt in them "And he that keepeth his commandments dwelleth in him, and he in him. And hereby we know that he abideth in us, by the Spirit which he hath given us. " 1 John 3:2

This will to obey is central to the definition of a Christian. The apostle John boldly states: "The man who says, 'I know him,' but does not do what he commands is a liar, and the truth is not in him. But if anyone obeys his word, God's love is truly made complete in him. This is how we know we are in him: Whoever claims to live in him must walk as Jesus did" 1 John 2:4-6. Enough said. No room for misinterpretation. Furthermore, Jesus said that those who have not received this obedient spirit from God will respond to His commands in a totally different way: "Isaiah was right when he prophesied about you hypocrites; as it is written: 'These people honor me with their lips, but their hearts are far from me. They worship me in vain; their teachings are but rules taught by men. ' You have let go of the commands of God and are holding on to the traditions of men" Mark 7:6-8. Devoid of obedience it is easy to manipulate the Word and dress it up to say what you want it to say according to your own selfish desires and your own ego. Those who have not totally yielded or do not have God's Spirit find it easy and convenient to disregard the biblical instructions they dislike. They devise their own traditions, giving the appearance of obeying and honoring God while sidestepping the intent of His instructions. This is why in our day a church feels justified in charging admission. Jesus said such worship is useless and empty. "Such people have eyes that can't see and ears that can't hear" Romans 11:8. God's Spirit is what gives believers the unction to willingly and faithfully obey His commandments "And the dragon was wroth with the woman, and went to make war with the remnant of her seed, which keep the commandments of God, and have the testimony of Jesus Christ. "Revelation 12:17. They have received from Him the power of the Holy Spirit to combat Satan and their own nature. In short, early Christians were transformed special people of God. They were a special people to God. This is where the church Jesus promised began; with the people. Knowing this, Jesus declared to His disciples that no one could serve two masters yet; Christians have spent massive amounts of time exploring ways to prove Jesus wrong. Having our cake and eating it too is so prevalent in our time we have told ourselves we can indeed have both; the things of God and the things of this world. Living our lives no differently than the world, it is no surprise non-believers stay away from the church in droves. Perhaps the only difference between believers and non believers can be seen in the regular church attendance of the believer. We feed our spirits the same media influences, we pursue the same commercial and materialistic desires, and we participate in the same revelries the world has to offer. But the church was not originally like that. The set of principles and values of the early Christians rejected the world's standards of honors and riches. Instead the Kingdom of which they were a part had a different master and it was only His voice to which they listened.

Several works were written to describe Christians to the Romans. These descriptions of early believers imply that having Christ and the world does not mix. These writers believed the early Christians to be fools. They did not identify with Christians who were afraid of torment after they die yet they did not fear torment from the Romans. Early Christians were taunted because they insisted on living a life that glorified their God. They worked hard were sometimes cold and hungry, and they were ruled by the Romans. No one in the Roman Empire could figure out how God could allow this. They believed Him to be weak and unable to assist His people.

Learning this about the early Christians makes it painfully obvious that the Christians of our day are wimpy to say the least. No one would accuse Christians today of ignoring what the world has to offer to look for a more kingdom mindset. Instead Christians today are accused of being hypocrites because we preach one thing and do another.

Besides being totally sold out for Jesus another characteristic indicative of the early Christians was their ability for unconditional love. During the first three centuries the entire church was immersed in the love each believer had for their fellow man; even those who were their enemies. Because of Jesus and His message people came together.

Jesus had said, "Love your enemies . . and pray for those who spitefully use you and persecute you". The early Christians accepted this statement as a command from their Lord, rather than as an ideal that couldn't be actually practiced in real life. Therefore, they did just that. They loved-unconditionally and Christianity spread throughout the ancient world without the help of a horde of missionary and evangelism programs. All it took was love just as Jesus had said.

Trusting God was a way of life for early Christians. Early Christians believed that even if obedience to God entailed great suffering, God was trustworthy to bring you through it. They didn't just hear the Word they lived the Word. With childlike, literal obedience to the teachings of Jesus and the apostles, early Christians were not concerned with understanding the reason for a commandment before they would obey it. They just trusted that God's way was always the best way. In their minds it would be irreverent to disbelieve God and demand explanations from God as from men. On the contrary, we always want to question God. We need a sign to obey what He has told us to do; especially if it goes against the status quo. Can you imagine Noah asking God why? Christians of this day were willing to suffer unspeakable horrors and to die rather than disown their God. Non believers suspected Christianity to be a force to be reckoned with if it meant that much to Christians. This unwavering commitment became the single most effective evangelistic tool for Christians. They were convinced the church would live on. They were not afraid of the consequences of holding on to their faith even if it meant they would suffer imprisonment and maybe even death. God was their protector.

The profound change God expects of Christians – conversion- is what we see exhibited in the Christians in biblical days. It is a miraculous shift in thinking and behavior. Would today's Christians be willing to suffer such persecution? Would we be able to endure harsh treatment and even death in the name of our God? Because we've allowed prayer to be taken out of schools, we've neglected to seek God's face on a daily basis, we've refused to humble ourselves and turn from our wicked ways it remains t be seen where our faith truly lies.

This look back at the early church should assist us in seeing how far we've strayed from the original Christians and the original church. We are nothing more than a watered down version; a mere shadow of what use to be. We know the Scripture, we know the prayers, we know the verbiage of religion but do we know the walk?

Traditions or Scripture

"Then came unto Him the Pharisees, and certain of the scribes, which came from Jerusalem. And when they saw some of His disciples eat bread with defiled, that is to say unwashen, hands, they found fault. " Mark 7:1-2

I remember asking this question a while back. Where in the Bible does it say a ministry needs a covering or that everyone in the church must "catch" the pastor's vision? Needless to say I never got any responses because I also asked that I not be given opinions, only book, chapter, and verse. Now, I am sure others would say, "Well, you never asked me. " But it was in an open forum on more than one occasion in full view of plenty of people who could have answered. The point is these types of quotes are repeated time and time again as if they were direct commands from the Lord.

Now it goes without saying that Paul was a mentor to Timothy, however, there is no mention of the fact that he was any type of covering. Nor does it indicate that Paul ever told Timothy when and where he could minister to the people. Nevertheless, people use this scripture frequently to wield controlling authority over persons called by God into the ministry creating more of a dictator role as opposed to a mentor role.

Pharisees were often the most vocal and influential religion in Jesus' day. The name Pharisee in its Hebrew form means separatists, or the separated ones. They were also known as chasidim, which means loyal to God, or loved of God - ironic because by the time Jesus came on the scene, they made themselves the most bitter and deadly opponents of Him and His message.

Unlike the Sadducees who were more affluent, the Pharisees were mostly middle-class businessmen, and therefore held a closer relationship with the common man. The Pharisees were more highly regarded by the common man than the Sadducees. Though they were a minority in the Sanhedrin and held a minority number of positions as priests, they basically controlled the decision making of the Sanhedrin far more than the Sadducees did primarily because they had the support of the people.

The inspired Word of God was a central piece of the religious beliefs of the Pharisees but they also gave equal authority to oral tradition. They attempted to defend this position by saying it went all the way back to Moses.

Evolving over the centuries, these traditions added to God's Word, which is forbidden in Deuteronomy 4:2 and the Pharisees sought to strictly obey these tra-

ditions along with the Old Testament. In fact,, the Gospels are full of examples where the Pharisees treated
their own traditions as equal to God's Word. Then John's
disciples came and asked him, Then came to him the
disciples of John, saying, Why do we and the Pharisees
fast oft, but thy disciples fast not? Matthew 9:14 Then
some Pharisees and teachers of the law came to Jesus
from Jerusalem and asked, "Why do your disciples break
the tradition of the elders? They don't wash their hands
before they eat!" Jesus replied, "And why do you break
the command of God for the sake of your tradition? For
God said, 'Honor your father and mother' and 'Anyone
who curses their father or mother is to be put to death.
' But you say that if anyone declares that what might
have been used to help their father or mother is 'devoted to God,' they are not to 'honor their father or mother' with it. Thus you nullify the word of God for the sake
of your tradition. You hypocrites! Isaiah was right when
he prophesied about you: "These people honor me with
their lips, but their hearts are far from me. They wor-

ship me in vain; their teachings are merely human rules. "Matthew 15:1-9 But all their works they do for to be seen of men: they make broad their phylacteries, and enlarge the borders of their garments," Matthew 23:5

Woe unto you, ye blind guides, which say, whosoever shall swear by the temple, it is nothing; but whosoever shall swear by the gold of the temple, he is a debtor! Matthew 23:16

The Pharisees and some of the teachers of the law who had come from Jerusalem gathered around Jesus and saw some of his disciples eating food with hands that were defiled, that is, unwashed. The Pharisees and all the Jews do not eat unless they give their hands a ceremonial washing, holding to the tradition of the elders. "When they come from the marketplace they do not eat unless they wash. And they observe many other traditions, such as the washing of cups, pitchers and kettles. So the Pharisees and teachers of the law asked Jesus, "Why don't your disciples live according to the tradition of the elders instead of eating their food with defiled hands?" He replied, "Isaiah was right when he prophesied about you hypocrites; as it is written: "These people honor me with their lips, but their hearts are far from me. They worship me in vain; their teachings are merely human rules. 'You have let go of the commands of God and are holding on to human traditions. "And he continued, "You have a fine way of setting aside the commands of God in order to observe your own traditions! For Moses said, 'Honor your father and mother,' and, 'Anyone who curses their father or mother is to be put to death. ' But you say that if anyone declares that what might have been used to help their father or mother is Corban that is, devoted to God— then you no longer let them do anything for their father or mother. Thus you nullify the word of God by your tradition that you have handed down. And you do many things like that. "Again Jesus called the crowd to him and said, "Listen to me, everyone, and understand this. Nothing outside a person can defile them by going into them. Rather, it is what comes out of a person that defiles them. "After he had left the crowd and entered the house, his disciples asked him about this parable. "Are you so dull?" he asked. "Don't you see that nothing that enters a person from the outside can defile them? For it does not go into their heart but into their stomach, and then out of the body. " In saying this, Jesus declared all foods clean. He went on: "What comes out of a person is what defiles them. For it is from within, out of a person's heart, that evil thoughts come—sexual immorality, theft, murder, adultery, greed, malice, deceit, lewdness, envy, slander, arrogance and folly. All these evils come from inside and defile a person. " Mark 7:1-23 "But woe unto you, Pharisees! for ye tithe mint and rue and all manner of herbs, and pass over judgment and the love of God: these ought ye to have done, and not to leave the other undone. " Luke 11:42. Despite consistent differences between the Pharisees and Sadducees there was one thing they had in common, contempt for Jesus. They had decided His constant interference in their status quo meant He had to go. They managed to set aside their differences long enough for the trial of Christ. It was at this point that the Sadducees and Pharisees united to put Christ to death And they led Jesus away to the high priest: and with him were assembled all the chief priests and the elders and the scribes. " Mark 14:53 "And straightway in the morning the chief priests held a consultation with the elders and scribes and the whole council, and bound Jesus, and carried him away, and delivered him to Pilate. " Mark15:1 If we let him thus alone, all men will believe on him: and the Romans shall come and take away both our place and nation. And one of them, named Caiaphas, being the high priest that same year, said unto them, Ye know nothing at all, Nor consider that it is expedient for us, that one man should die for the people, and that the whole nation perish not. John 11:48-50.

Perhaps obeying God is what the Pharisees meant to do, but eventually they became so caught up and engrossed in minute parts of The Law plus all the rules and regulations they themselves added to it that they became blind to The Messiah when He was walking among them. They saw His miracles, they heard His Words, but instead of receiving it with exceeding gladness, they did all they could to stop Him. The culmination of their efforts was getting Him killed because He claimed to be the Son of God.

In Jesus' day it is fair to say that the boundaries separating the people were real. The biggest of these was the boundary between Jew and non-Jew. For many there was no getting around this particular boundary because the Jewish people had so often faced total annihilation by non-Jews.

So the Jewish people at the time of Jesus held on to their uniqueness at all costs. In their minds, their very existence as a nation relied on their uniqueness which included three things; the circumcision of their men, their observance of the Jewish Sabbaths, and their purity laws. Many Jewish people indeed faced martyrdom rather than give up those rituals and traditions they believed set them apart as the people of God.

In the minds of the Jewish people the only way non-Jewish people could be welcomed was if they adhered to these ideals. Pious Jews believed everyone else was unclean, impure, contaminated. Mutual hostility resulted in violence between Jews and non-Jews. Jesus however was Jewish. He was born into a Jewish family, a descendant of the ancient King David, from the tribe of Judah, a descendant of Abraham, the father of the Jewish people. He was circumcised as a baby, and he grew up observing the things that maintained the uniqueness of the Jewish people.

But when he began his ministry, he questioned and challenged many of the traditional ways of understanding. For Jesus, being the people of God wasn't about ceremony and tradition.

Therefore it happened on this particular day that a religious delegation had been assigned to evaluate the ministry of Jesus in an effort to protect the people of Israel from a false prophet. Yet instead of evaluating against the measure of God's Word they chose to evaluate Him against their religious traditions. This entire encounter focused on the ritual washing of the hands; a ceremony mandated for priests before entering the tabernacle. The type of hand washing they were speaking of involved an elaborate ceremony that included a special prayer. These washings were part of the oral tradition, mans interpretation of the law written down, not by Scripture. The leaders knew this was not Scriptural but they criticized the disciples anyway. In this debate Jesus questions the traditions of the Pharisees, the rules and rituals that they added to the Old Testament law. Jesus points out to theses men there is a difference in traditions and its religious practices. Jesus says that is what he came for. Jesus came to establish a relationship with Him, so one could worship the Father not the traditions of the past. Being religious means it is an end in itself. Christianity is a means to an end, a relationship with Jesus Christ. That is the difference between Jesus and the scribes and Pharisees. The Pharisees turned what was supposed to be worship of God into an end in and of itself. They were religious for religious sake.

Much like the religious leaders of that time who honored the oral law more than the written law, many of our religious leaders today have developed interpretations and applications of the law to govern their local "denominations" however, many of these ceremonial edicts are not Scriptural requirements that will lead one to Christ. The church is being used to escape the truth of the gospel, the worship of God. Religious leaders are using the law of men to gain respect, position, and wealth. They are using the law to have power over people, instead of showing the people how the law can help them to find God in their lives Because Jesus did not corroborate the validity of the oral law of the Jews He became the object of attack. Because He did not sign off on the "traditions" of man He became a scapegoat. When re-

Killing Religion

ferring to religious leaders who upheld man's traditions over God's will Jesus called them hypocrites. In fact,, it was not uncommon for Jesus to call the religious leaders of the day hypocrites every time he saw them. What does this say? It simply says in matters like these we are way too concerned with trivial ideas and issues instead of being concerned with the saving of souls. Does God really command all of the rules and regulations placed on believers; rules regarding a certain type of attire or a specific education? God is saying they do all these things attend church, read their Bible, contribute money, do ministry, but their hearts are far from me. Are these commandments of God or traditions of men and their religion?

Satan is successful in deceiving us this way for good reason. The apostle Paul explains that the natural mind of man—the mind that is not guided by God's Spirit—cannot always see the purpose behind God's laws. "But the natural man does not receive the things of the Spirit

76

of God, for they are foolishness tohim; nor can he know them, because they are spiritually discerned" 1 Corinthians 2:14.

However, most people are not overtly contrary toward many of God's laws. They usually recognize that killing and stealing are wrong. But, they are less inclined — perhaps without recognizing it—to embrace laws that challenge their own personal, natural way of thinking. In that sense disobeying God's laws appeals to people. Paul explains why disobedience can appeal to our basic instincts: "The carnal mind is enmity against God; for it is not subject to the law of God, nor indeed can be" Romans 8:7. The carnal mind not only lacks spiritual discernment, it resents God's authority as expressed in His laws.

The enemy is shrewd: he exploits human nature by swaying people to believe his deceptions. Satan retains just enough truth in his doctrines to persuade people they are following Christ. But he introduces sufficient error to prevent them from living the way that God requires. Therefore it becomes so easy to focus on tradition that we never bat an eye at the exclusion of others who don't keep the tradition. Eventually those excluded will become discouraged and turn away definitely from church and maybe even from God. We are so ready to follow the authority of humans yet we ignore plain teachings from the Word of God.

Later in this passage Jesus points out to the religious leaders how they ignore God's command to honor their father and mother by allowing one to say their possessions belong to God thereby making their possessions unavailable to help their parents; but they're concerned about hand washing which was never commanded in the first place. They had made the Word of God of no effect through tradition. These leaders only had an image of religion. Jesus plainly spoke and said it is not what goes in a man that defiles him but what comes out. How appropriate for us today. You will hear many say, 'I don't gamble, I don't smoke, I don't eat pork, I don't cuss,' however, those same "church folks" with their gossiping and backbiting sow discord among the brethren, which in Proverbs is said to be an abomination.

People often assume that whenever the term "Christian" is used those bearing the name are following after the precepts and examples laid down by Jesus. Jesus foretold that some would claim His name but deny Him by their actions. He said they would call Him Lord, Lord, but not do the things He said. He held that two religions would become known one led by the Spirit of Christ and another led by a different spirit. This imitation of the true church of God and its fake beliefs would lead many, even some true believers, away from the correct teachings of Jesus. Both would bear His name and would outwardly appear to be good, yet, one would only be established to capture the minds and hearts of humanity through insupportable religious customs that were neither approved nor practiced by Jesus.

So, where does this false distorted truth come from? If not from Scripture where do most Christian religions get their teachings and practices?

Let's take another look at the beginnings of the early church. Even as the apostles went about establishing believers among the nations, the enemy was at work producing an alternative Christian religion to what the apostles were creating. A religion that looked Christian on the outside but had a different agenda. New and different doctrines were cunningly introduced. Some even began challenging and contradicting the teachings of Christ's apostles. Paul warned, "For there are many insubordinate, both idle talkers and deceivers, especially those of the circumcision, whose mouths must be stopped, who subvert whole households, teaching things which they ought not, for the sake of dishonest gain" Titus 1:10-11. Because of these tactics Paul told Timothy to look into the backgrounds, knowledge, and character of anyone who wanted to be ordained. "

"Since an overseer manages God's household, he must be blameless, not overbearing, not quick-tempered, not given to drunkenness, not violent, not pursuing dishonest gain. Rather, he must be hospitable, one who loves what is good, who is self-controlled, upright, holy and disciplined. He must hold firmly to the trustworthy message as it has been taught, so that he can encourage others by sound doctrine and refute those who oppose it. " verses 7-9.

Increasingly, "false apostles" began contradicting and undermining the teachings of the true apostles of Christ. Paul cautioned the church in Rome: Now I beseech you, brethren, mark them which cause divisions and offences contrary to the doctrine which ye have learned; and avoid them. For they that are such serve not our Lord Jesus Christ, but their own belly; and by good words and fair speeches deceive the hearts of the simple. For your obedience is come abroad unto all men. I am glad therefore on your behalf: but yet I would have you wise unto that which is good, and simple concerning evil. " Romans 16:17-19. False doctrines from competing religious leaders, masquerading as ministers of Christ, sprang up "in opposition to" Christ's apostles and his faithful servants. Jewish leaders were at the forefront. However it was not long before false teachers emerged from people of other backgrounds within the Church as well. The dissident doctrines that eventually grew to influence people the most were a blend of pagan and misguided Jewish philosophies combined with the mysticism popular at that time. For example, Christians in the Roman province of Galatia turned in large numbers from the teachings of the apostle Paul and to a corrupted, cunningly devised but fake gospel promoted by these false apostles.

Paul described the approach they used and the effect the false teachers had on Christians in Galatia. I marvel that you are turning away so soon from Him who called you in the grace of Christ, to a different gospel, which is not another; but there are some who trouble you and want to pervert the gospel of Christ Galatians 1:6-7.

Because they were being swept into the many sects making up the emerging false religion Paul had to contend with religious strife generated by Jewish and gentile elements amongst the Galatian congregations.

Without outright rejecting the gospel Paul taught cunning pretenders simply perverted certain aspects of it. Then they seduced the Galatian Christians into accepting their gospel—a lethal concoction of truth and error. It contained enough truth to appear righteous and Christian, but it contained sufficient error to prevent any who would accept it from receiving salvation.

I often wonder if we have continued this practice into our present day religions; particularly when I look at the number of people in the church who are hurting; those who need deliverance and salvation but who rarely receive it because the "church" judges, condemns, or otherwise runs them away.

Notice Paul's blistering condemnation of that "different" gospel: "But even if we, or an angel from heaven, preach any other gospel to you than what we have preached to you, let him be accursed. As we have said before, so now I say again, if anyone preaches any other gospel to you than what you have received, let him be accursed" verses 8-9. If it is not a gospel of reconciliation, if it is not a gospel of deliverance, if it is not a gospel of salvation, it is not the gospel.

This controversy over God's law erupted within the Church as soon as the first gentiles were converted. Certain Jewish believers wanted to force circumcision and other physical requirements on the gentiles. They demanded that gentile converts be physically circumcised to receive salvation "And certain men which came down from Judaea taught the brethren, and said, Except ye be circumcised after the manner of Moses, ye cannot be saved. " Acts 15:1. Similar to what we do today in our various denominations. In a major conference in Jerusalem, the apostles and elders determined that physical circumcision should not be regarded as a requirement for gentiles' salvation "When therefore Paul and Barnabas had no small dissension and disputation with them, they determined that Paul and Barnabas, and certain other of them, should go up to Jerusalem unto the apostles and elders about this question. " Acts 15:2 But there rose up certain of the sect of the Pharisees which believed, saying, "That it was needful to circumcise them, and to command them to keep the law of Moses. And the apostles and elders came together for to consider of this matter. And when there had been much disputing, Peter rose up, and said unto them, Men and brethren, ye know how that a good while ago God made choice among us, that the Gentiles by my mouth should hear the word of the gospel, and believe. And God, which knoweth the hearts, bare them witness, giving them the Holy Ghost, even as he did unto us, And put no difference between us and them, purifying their hearts by faith. Now therefore why tempt ye God, to put a yoke upon the neck of the disciples, which neither our fathers nor we were able to bear?" Acts15:5-10. Peter noted that God had recently given the Holy Spirit to several gentiles without their being circumcised, demonstrating His will in the matter "And the apostles and brethren that were in Judaea heard that the Gentiles had also received the word of God. And when Peter was come up to Jerusalem, they that were of the circumcision contended with him, Saying, Thou wentest in to men uncircumcised, and didst eat with them. But Peter rehearsed the matter from the beginning, and expounded it by order unto them, saying," Acts 11:1-4 "And as I began to speak, the Holy Ghost fell on them, as on us at the beginning. Then remembered I the word of the Lord, how that he said, John indeed baptized with water; but ye shall be baptized with the Holy Ghost. Forasmuch then as God gave them the like gift as he did unto us, who believed on the Lord Jesus Christ; what was I, that I could withstand God? When they heard these things, they held their peace, and glorified God, saying, then hath God also to the Gentiles granted repentance unto life." Acts 11:15-18. The same Jews also demanded that gentiles observe the temple ceremonies and rituals, which pointed to greater spiritual realities such as the sacrifice of Christ. The apostles insisted that Christ's sacrifice was sufficient for the forgiveness of sins through the grace of God "For such an high priest became us, who is holy, harmless, undefiled, separate from sinners, and made higher than the heavens; Who needeth not daily, as those high priests, to offer up sacrifice, first for his own sins, and then for the people's: for this he did once, when he offered up himself." Hebrews 7:26-27. "The temple sacrifices and rituals were only temporary institutions until the sacrifice of the real "Lamb of God" The next day John seeth Jesus coming unto him, and saith, Behold the Lamb of God, which taketh away the sin of the world. " John 1:29 and His work in the lives of believers. The apostles taught that they were no longer required But we believe that through the grace of the LORD Jesus Christ we shall be saved, even as they. Acts 15:11 Then verily the first covenant had also ordinances of divine service, and a worldly sanctuary. For there was a tabernacle made; the first, wherein was the candlestick, and the table, and the shewbread; which is called the sanctuary. And after the second veil, the tabernacle which is called the Holiest of all; Which had the golden censer, and the ark of the covenant overlaid round about with gold, wherein was the golden pot that had manna, and Aaron's rod that budded, and the tables of the covenant; And over it the cherubims of glory shadowing the mercy seat; of which we cannot now speak particularly. Now when these things were thus ordained, the priests went always into the first tabernacle, accomplishing the service of God. But into the second went the high priest alone once every year, not without blood, which he offered for himself, and for the errors of the people: The Holy Ghost this signifying, that the way into the holiest of all was not yet made manifest, while as the first tabernacle was yet standing: Which was a figure for the time then present, in which were offered both gifts and sacrifices, that could not make him that did the service perfect, as pertaining to the conscience; Which stood only in meats and drinks, and divers washings, and carnal ordinances, imposed on them until the time of reformation. But Christ being come an high priest of good things to come, by a greater and more perfect tabernacle, not made with hands, that is to say, not of this building; Neither by the blood of goats and calves, but by his own blood he entered in once into the holy place, having obtained eternal redemption for us. For if the blood of bulls and of goats, and the ashes of an heifer sprinkling the unclean, sanctifieth to the purifying of the flesh: How much more shall the blood of Christ, who through the eternal Spirit offered himself without spot to God, purge your conscience from dead works to serve the living God? And for this cause he is the mediator of the new testament, that by means of death, for the redemption of the transgressions that were under the first testament, they which are called might receive the promise of eternal inheritance. Hebrews 9:1-15 because they were concerned only with foods and drinks, various washings, and fleshly ordinances imposed until the time of reformation Hebrews 9:10. But the apostles never regarded God's spiritual laws, summarized by the Ten Commandments, as being in the same category with "fleshly ordinances. " They always supported obedience to God's commandments. Paul made this clear: "Circumcision is nothing and uncircumcision is nothing, but keeping the commandments of God is what matters" 1 Corinthians 7:19. He concluded: "Do we then make void the law through faith? Certainly not! On the contrary, we establish the law" Romans 3:31.

Peter anticipated that not just a few—but many—Christians would turn aside from the truth to follow doctrines that were more appealing to the carnal mind. Later John confirms that this is indeed what happened: "They went out from us, but they were not of us; for if they had been of us, they would have continued with us; but they went out that they might be made manifest, that none of them were of us" 1 John 2:19. "Teaching them to observe all things whatsoever I have commanded you: and, lo, I am with you always, even unto the end of the world. Amen. Matthew 28:20 Jesus commands His disciples to teach the people everything he had commanded them to. He was not at all pleased with the replacing of God's commandments with traditions and human reason. Like Jesus, Paul also warned that we should not accept traditions as replacements.

Nevertheless, a divided and unconverted form of religion has emerged. This squabbling bitterly divided new brand of religious fervor has rapidly expanded and become the visible Christian church. Claiming to offer salvation, but without the necessity of true repentance, it holds just enough truth to appeal to a majority of the people.

The origin of this religion rests with the rise to power of the Emperor Constantine. He had many enemies, and his political position remained insecure. In all the empire, only Christians were unaligned politically. Immediately seeing an opportunity to use this formerly persecuted and politically alienated religious body to strengthen his position Constantine went to work.

First he legalized Christianity. Then, only two years later, he called all the divided professing Christian groups together to come into agreement on a unified system of belief. He wanted a united religious body that was politically committed to him.

Constantine presided over doctrinal deliberations and dictated statements of belief whenever disagreements could not be ironed out. In this way the "church" would no longer be persecuted by its enemies but now it would be governed by the Roman Empire.

In its haste to add members and new converts this new religion allowed new practices to be introduced. As such the task of correcting and getting rid of some of the superstitions and pagan practices that infiltrated became an undertaking for the future rather than the present. Obviously this correction never took place. They simply dressed up the paganism with a religious coat. The end result a strange mix of beliefs, practices, and customs that barely resemble original Christianity. This religion the apostles of Jesus fought so hard against grew and gained popularity. Eventually it fragmented into competing denominations that never completely returned to the original practices and teachings of Jesus. "One Lord, one faith, one baptism" this is what scripture says. However, everyone who possesses the Holy Spirit does not necessarily listen to it. Therefore, Christianity has become fragmented due to the crab like mentality that creates competition in the body of Christ. Too often those wearing the label Christian have not been truly converted. They have not had a transformative change of heart. They have been saved but not delivered.

The Bible is clear. There is nothing uncertain about the deity of Christ, heaven and hell, or salvation by grace through faith. Nevertheless, many have taken verses out of their immediate context and failed to understand the historical/cultural context which has caused great damage. Ignorance to the whole Word of God has created chaos and confusion. Much like Apollos who was an eloquent preacher, yet, he delivered an incomplete message because he only knew of the baptism of John. He was uninformed about Jesus and His provision of salvation.

The reality is, what God really wants from us is our heart. Our change must come from the inside out. The wonder working power of God must be at work on the inside or our "church" isn't real.

God enjoys the way we use what He has given us to worship and to serve Him as we edify our neighbor. In some ways, this freedom to live in the principle of the law is more difficult than living by the letter of the law. Living by the letter of the law is easier because it is all spelled out in black and white. We don't have to take any responsibility for our own actions, if we follow the law that is great; if we cannot follow the law it is ok because we can always say it is a bad law. But when we are given the freedom to express the principle of the law in our own way, then we have to take full responsibility for our actions. We stand alone before God. We cannot blame anyone or anything for our failure to act, or for our failure for acting wrong. But it is in that freedom we find the grace of God.

More often than not however many hide behind a façade of spiritual superiority; pretentious intellectual fronts that attempt to cover up insecurities, weaknesses or secret sins. Hiding behind a mask of legalism is discouraged by the Spirit of the living God. Paul wrote, "Since you died with Christ to the basic principles of this world, why, as though you still belong to it, do you submit to its rulers. Do not handle. Do not taste. Do not touch. These are all destined to perish with use, because they are based on human commands and teachings. Such regulations indeed have the appearance of wisdom, but they lack any value in restraining sensual indulgence. Set your hearts on things above, not on earthly things. Colossians 2:20-3:1-2 We need to be more responsive to the chastening of the Lord when we drift into a defensive Pharisaical spirituality. As the "church" we should be asking God to help us rid ourselves of anything that keeps us from a real relationship with Him. That includes rules regulations and traditions that hinder our allegiance to Him. The true believer should have one thing and one thing only on their mind and that is a real relationship with God. No false dependencies, no legalism, just God. Paul wrote, "For I resolved to know nothing while I was with you except Jesus Christ and Him crucified. I came to you in weakness and fear, and with much trembling." I Corinthians 2:2-3 Ask the Lord to help you set aside all of your false fronts to allow Him to transform you into a whole person fashioned after Christ. Be careful not to allow the customs and traditions of men to rule your life as opposed to holding high the cross. The World wants you to look good on the outside but God wants you to look good on the inside. It won't matter if you dressed the part. It won't matter if you finished a degree. In the end the only thing that will matter is your relationship with God. We must be freed from the tyranny of the externals so that we may enjoy a freedom to live with the law of love in our hearts. It is great to clean your hands, but how about your heart?

THE CHURCH TODAY

So what is the Church?

"And when he was demanded of the Pharisees, when the kingdom of God should come, he answered them and said, "The kingdom of God cometh not with observation: Neither shall they say, Lo here! Or lo there! For, behold, the kingdom of God is within you. " Luke 17:20-21

Social mecca's, networking centers; churches today are redefining themselves in hopes of gaining new members. But what does the Bible say the Church should be doing? At the dawn of the 21st century, does the Church still have a purpose? Can you have a part in it?

"Mainstream religion" is having an identity crisis. Many who consider themselves Christians don't really know or understand the purpose of the church or religion. They really can't place a value on its role in their lives. Some yearn for the comfortable traditions of the past. Others seek a more "authentic" experience. Some just search for healing and comfort. But what is the purpose of the church?

Disillusioned with "organized religion," many are looking elsewhere for answers. For them, religion has become largely irrelevant, because their church has no meaningful identity or role.

Why are churches so confused? What is the purpose of the church in the first place? And what should your church be doing today? What is religion and what is its role?

We don't go to church. We are the church. It is not

brick and mortar standing on a concrete foundation with steel beams and stained glass windows. It is not Methodism, Catholicism, Baptist, or Pentecostal. The people of God, who believe in Christ, we are the church, the body of Christ.

Our current understanding of the church as a building is misdirected because while it is important for us to assemble ourselves with one another for the edification of the body, the true biblical representation of the church does not indicate that it be done in a building. In fact, arguably the greatest sermon ever preached by Jesus, the Sermon on the Mount, was preached on the side of a mountain.

The word "church" comes from the Greek word ekklesia which is defined as "an assembly" or "called-out ones. " The root meaning of "church" is not that of a building, but of a people. In Romans 16:5, Likewise greet the church that is in their house. Salute my well-beloved Epaenetus, who is the firstfruits of Achaia unto Christ,

Paul refers to the church in their house—not a church building, but a body of believers.

The church of which Jesus is the head is one that includes a body of believers who have been filled with His Spirit as is evidenced in Ephesians 1:22-23 which says, "And God placed all things under his feet and appointed him to be head over everything for the church, which is his body, the fullness of him who fills everything in every way." From the day of Pentecost until the coming again of Jesus, the body of believers is what makes up the true church and our charge is to bring others into the knowledge of Jesus and who He is plain and simple.

Having explained what the "true church" is, it is now necessary to talk about the assembly. Once we have accepted Jesus as our personal savior we all become part of the universal church. "For by one Spirit are we all baptized into one body, whether we be Jews or Gentiles, whether we be bond or free; and have been all made to drink into one Spirit." 1 Corinthians 12:13.

Cheryl Lacey Donovan

Furthermore Hebrews 10:25 says, "Not forsaking the assembling of ourselves together, as the manner of some
is; but exhorting one another: and so much the more,
as ye see the day approaching. " This reminds us of the
importance of assembling ourselves together for the
purpose of edification and exhortation. As people of
the universal body of Christ, we should seek fellowship
and edification in a local assembly of believers. It is here
where we as members of the body should be able to apply the principles of 1 Corinthians 12:13: encouraging,
teaching, and building one another up in the knowledge
and grace of the Lord Jesus Christ. However we must
exercise due diligence in our choice of assembly by ad-
hering to the admonition of Paul when He told Timothy
to study to show himself approved. We should refer to
1 John 4:1-5 "Beloved, believe not every spirit, but try
the spirits whether they are of God: because many false
prophets are gone out into the world. Hereby know ye
the Spirit of God: Every spirit that confesseth that Jesus
Christ is come in the flesh is of God: And every spirit that

105

confesseth not that Jesus Christ is come in the flesh is not of God: and this is that spirit of antichrist, whereof ye have heard that it should come; and even now already is it in the world. Ye are of God, little children, and have overcome them: because greater is he that is in you, than he that is in the world. They are of the world: therefore speak they of the world, and the world heareth them." This tells us not to believe every spirit but try the spirits whether they are of God before we align ourselves with any particular assembly. We should liken ourselves to the Berean Jews in Acts 17:11 who were willingly receptive to the Word of God and because of their great eagerness examined Scripture everyday to see if what Paul said was true. Because they honestly listened and compared what they heard to Old Testament Scripture which is all they had at the time many were led to faith in Jesus as the Messiah. This fervor extended itself beyond the synagogue walls and permeated into the Greek men and women of Berea. The Berean's are a good example of how the assembly of God's people should be carried out today. We are called to eagerly learn from the Word of God no matter who the teacher is and to investigate new teaching in comparison to the Bible. Theirs is a model for those who desire to grow spiritually today.

Religion or Relationship

Over 90% of the world's population practices one religion or another. Rules and rituals are the two ingredients common to all of them. The issue: many of these religions tend to believe to a certain degree that adherence to the rules will make a person right with God. Conversely some religions observe rituals rather than obeying a list of rules. They believe performing these tasks or participating in this service will bring one closer to God.

Religion is something you do over and over, continuously. It is your rituals, your customs, and your habitual activities. Even the devil is religious.

The Bible says, "He walks about as a roaring lion seeking whom he can devour" 1 Peter 5:8 He is religiously going around looking for folks he can defeat. But relationship is something altogether different. Relationship is a connection, an association between you and something else. Relationship is the connection that exists between you and someone else. Relationship is the companionship that exists between you and those that you are close to.

And in order to have relationship, there must first be a fellowship. It is necessary for you to have more than religion when it comes to God. You need more than repetitive habitual set of tasks you perform Sunday after Sunday. You need a relationship with God.

It is a dangerous proposition to have just religion and no relationship. When you only have religion and not a relationship, it becomes difficult to handle the storms of life because the enemy causes you to believe you are all alone. You won't be able to deal with the tough times because you won't know that in order to have a victory you must go through a battle. You won't be able to persevere in the midst of adversity because you won't know that weeping only endures for a short time and that God can wipe away all tears. Your faith will become faulty. Your praise will become passive. Your witness will become weak. Your testimony will become tired and worn.

Christ or Christianity

Right after the crucifixion of Jesus there was a man named Saul who struck fear in the hearts of every Christian. In Saul's mind the only good Christian was a dead Christian. Saul was there and gave his endorsement of the stoning of Stephen who came to be known as the first saint.

Acts chapter 9 records that one day, while Saul was on one of his way to wreak havoc in the lives of more Christians, as he was nearing Damascus, he suddenly found himself surrounded by a very bright light. He fell to the ground and heard a voice from heaven say to him,

"Saul, Saul, why do you persecute Me?

The voice was of Jesus Christ Himself. Saul's meeting with Jesus that day caused him to realize the errors of his ways. Paul, as he came to be known after his Damascus Road experience, accepted Christianity was not a threat to the Jews, but rather the fulfillment of all they hold true. Saul, like most of us had reached his day of conversion He was literally knocked down on the road to Damascus and directly called by God.

Paul is by far one of my favorite faith siblings. He explained his adherence to the precepts of the Pharisees this way: Brethren, my heart's desire and prayer to God for Israel is, that they might be saved. For I bear them record that they have a zeal of God, but not according to knowledge. For they being ignorant of God's righteousness, and going about to establish their own righteousness, have not submitted themselves unto the righteousness of God. Romans 10:1-3. Blinded by self righteousness Paul persecuted the church. A devout

Pharisee scholar, Paul was very well versed in all of the laws and principles of the Jewish religion. He was sincere, but he was sincerely wrong. Christ did not come to form a religion instead he came to save a people. Religion today is full of people much like Paul before his conversion. Sincere but lacking in the righteousness of God they simply don't believe they can be wrong.

I will never forget a conversation I had with one such "Christian brother." He began to talk about a young man he had seen in church earlier that day. He was irate about the fact that this young man had come to church with a doo rag on his head. He relayed to those of us listening how he had chastised this young man for his "church fashion" faux pas.

The interesting thing about this conversation is that I happen to know this "church brothers" background. He has been in and out of legal trouble for credit card theft. Now, I have yet to read in Scripture where it says thou shalt not wear a doo rag, but I do know the Word says thou shalt not steal. Exodus 20:15. Was this "Christian brother" more concerned about having the mind of Christ or was he more concerned with his Christian principles? Why do we judge and condemn the conduct of others and go so easy on ourselves? What does God have to say to us about this peculiar tendency? "And why beholdest thou the mote that is in thy brother's eye, but considerest not the beam that is in thine own eye? Or how wilt thou say to thy brother, Let me pull out the mote out of thine eye; and, behold, a beam is in thine own eye?" Thou hypocrite, first cast out the beam out of thine own eye; and then shalt thou see clearly to cast out the mote out of thy brother's eye. Matthew 7:3-5. With precious little real information and with an absurd confidence in his 'character radar' this "Christian brother made a judgment about someone else. This judgment which was made way too early to be reliable is known as a pre-judgment or prejudice. It was basically made on the way this young man, who came to church that day, looked.

God wants us to realize how unhealthy it is to live a critical lifestyle, how He distains such an attitude to life. In Matthew 7:3-5 God strongly admonishes us not to be condemning of others.

Membership or Discipleship

"Therefore go and make disciples of all nations, baptizing them in the name of the Father and of the Son and of the Holy Spirit. " Matthew 28:19

Today's churches are scrambling to find their meaning. The true mission of churches is often hidden behind impressive numbers, energetic fellowship, and self-help programs in a casual atmosphere. Instead of identifying their truth in the Word they seek to find their job description in surveys, questionnaires, and feedback forms that list answers such as too boring, too traditional, and too contemporary as responses to the question "How was your church experience. Often these churches lack true disciples among their members. If a crowd is what you want this may be the place to be but if true experiential relationship is what you are after you may need to keep looking.

Fragmented "mini-churches" are not much better. As these new religious organizations splinter and proliferate, confusion grows about the meaning and purpose of the Church.

The role of God's true church is not a mystery. There is no need for confusion. Those seeking to be a part of the church Jesus Christ built can be confident that if they are doing what He and His disciples did they are on the right track. It does not matter how our times may change, the social fads, trendy distractions, misleading doctrines, God and His intent for His church never changes and never will. God's true church will be proclaiming to the world the good news of Jesus Christ's coming Kingdom. And this gospel of the kingdom shall be preached in all the world for a witness unto all nations; and then shall the end come. Matthew 24:14. It will be blowing a bold clarion call of repentance and spiritual change. "Cry aloud, spare not; lift up your voice like a trumpet; tell My people their transgression, and the house of Jacob their sins" Isaiah 58:1. Even in the twenty first century, the church that Christ built will be following His example no matter the cost. Are you a part of that Church?

Christianities growth has become superficial at best because on many fronts it only calculates the number of members reflected on the church roles . In fact, the mandate to make disciples of men has become an afterthought which has seriously affected the mission of mainstream denominations.

However, discipleship is the mandate to which we are called as followers of Christ. Just to drive the point home, why are you asked to "join the church?" Is that

Scriptural or is that another tradition of men? Why would you need to join the church if you are the church? We are not called to be church members or part of a denomination; we are called to be one with Jesus.

In the same way a good social club member would perform, a good church member is one who goes to the gatherings, gives their cash, and takes an interest in the activities of the day. Church members, at best, are mere observers. Coming to church on Sunday is their main event. They come to sanctuary, sing a few melodies, recount a litany or two, put their offering in the plate and go home until the following Sunday; alternatively, a good disciple is something distinctively different.

Being a disciple is a lifestyle. Rescuing individuals from the kingdom of darkness and restoring them to God's kingdom through men and not gatherings or projects was God's unique arrangement. Jesus began this arrangement with His twelve disciples. He taught them about the Kingdom of God and utilized His life as an example and they likewise taught others. This is discipleship in its truest structure. They were doing the work of the ministry. "He gave some as apostles, and some as prophets, and some as evangelists, and some as pastors, and teachers, for the equipping of the saints for the work of the ministry. " Ephesians 4:11-12. To equip you through the process of Discipleship to be able to do the work of the ministry is the responsibility of the apostles, prophets, evangelists, pastors, teachers not to run institutional church work or deliver nice speeches on Sunday. Creating disciples not members; this is what we were called to do.

Jesus' mandate to make disciples of men should be the most important objective of the church. The Bible tells us what it means to follow Jesus. This is our ultimate mandate; to be more like Him and less like the world. Christ came to not only proclaim the coming of the Kingdom of God but to establish it. It wasn't by happenstance that Jesus was walking by the Sea of Galilee that fateful day. He was on a mission. It was a well planned out strategy; a kingdom search for those willing to remove themselves from all that was familiar to them and follow Him. This was a deliberate trip that would establish the framework of the Kingdom by calling His first supporters into administration. A risky non-traditional move since the standard was for the student to search out their instructor and request the chance to sit at his feet. This was his first lesson "whosoever will be chief among you let him be your servant. " Matthew 20:27The call to discipleship is personal. It involves a powerful transformation and a personal guarantee from Jesus to "make you" a fisher of men. It is a call to imitate Jesus in life and word. True disciples have two obligations: become like Jesus and pass on His teachings to others. Christ's intention, to spread Himself and His influence to a never ending group of disciples.

What you were before you received Christ is of little importance. Just look at His original disciples. Their backgrounds and characters were nothing special. In fact,, most of them would probably be ostracized by our church today. Nonetheless, Jesus chose them in spite of who they were and what they had done. As a result they became the organizers of the Christian church.

Christ met people on their own terms. He gave of himself to each of them regardless of their lifestyle. Discipleship not membership is what we've all been called to do. It is demonstrative. It is a call to serve. It must not be replaced with a call to church membership, denomination, or an organization.

THE END TIME CHURCH

Kingdom Living

The entire premise for this book is that we must get away from our man made traditions and turn to the scripture to identify what the end time church should be doing. Let's take a look at 2 Timothy. In it are great examples of how we can create God's kingdom here on earth.

Strength for the work of the ministry is a recurring theme throughout the Bible. In Timothy Paul encourages Timothy to have strength at least twenty-five times because Timothy was somewhat timid and easily discouraged. Isaiah 40:29-30 reminds us that God is always there to give us strength; "He gives power to the weak, and to those who have no might, He increases strength . . . those that wait on the LORD shall renew their strength". However, this strength is not something that comes easily. We have to receive and embrace it. Just as we must do weight training to increase our physical strength, so must we do weight training in the spirit through our consistently seeking Him and relying on Him instead of ourselves to become spiritually strong.

So where does this strength come from? Simply put God's grace. Paul told Timothy to be strong in the grace that is in Jesus. This strength in grace is essential for a strong Christian life. The unmerited favor of God towards us that is in Christ Jesus should give us a confidence and boldness we could never have if we lived our lives thinking we are on probation or that God hasn't made up His mind about us yet. There is nothing that can make us as strong as saying, "I know whose I am.

I am a child of God. I have the love and favor of God even though I don't deserve it." That is the strength that comes by grace. Paul knew what it was like to receive the strength of God's grace, as he explained in 2 Corinthians 12:9-10 And He said to me, "My grace is sufficient for you, for My strength is made perfect in weakness." Therefore most gladly I will rather boast in my infirmities, that the power of Christ may rest upon me." This wasn't what Paul had heard. This is what Paul knew because of his experiences and therefore, he was able to encourage Timothy.

After telling Timothy to be strong in grace, Paul admonished him to spread the word and commit it among faithful men. God gave ministry to us, not for us to keep, but for us to pass on to others. An essential part of our work especially if we are pastors is to pour into others what God has committed to us. It goes without saying that everything a pastor does in his ministry he should train others to do as well. This job of training leaders was so important that it could not be restricted to Timothy alone. Those whom he had trained must also be given the job to teach others also. There are no duties of a pastor so holy or so secret that he should keep them all to himself. He should always seek to spread ministry to any and everyone that will receive it, and to train others to do the work of the ministry. The idea here is that Timothy nor those in ministry today are to teach others their own particular ideas or theories, but rather simple Apostolic doctrine and example as Paul put it, the things that you have heard from me. What was poured into Timothy by Paul, he was now responsible for pouring into others. Training others for leadership and ministry is an integral part of a pastor's job description. He should not only train leaders when the need for a leader is obvious; nor should he only train leaders for the needs of his congregation alone. He should train leaders for the Kingdom of God in general, whether they are used in ministry at the particular pastor's congregation or not.

The type of training necessary for those in the kingdom is not for the faint at heart. It's not for those who are here today and gone tomorrow. In fact, Paul refers to soldier's athletes and farmers when he speaks of the tenacity and perseverance necessary to be a worker in the vineyard for the kingdom. Persevering and enduring hardship as a good soldier are both qualities necessary for those seeking to be effective witnesses and evangelists for Christ. This was not a suggestion from Paul it was a directive; a requirement. The interesting dynamic with relation to this command is that all of us want to claim the victory but we seldom want to go into battle. The reality is everyone will be involved in battle and we must be equipped for it when it comes. There is no victory without a battle and every battle is fought against an enemy. We are reminded of this truth when we read Ephesians which tells us that we don't battle against flesh and blood but against supernatural enemies commanded by the devil himself. No real soldier can expect to engage in battle without enduring hardship. Conversely no good soldier ever gives up because hardship comes. As believers if we are not willing to endure hardship then we will never accomplish much for Jesus Christ. They will give up as soon as something hard is required of them; they cannot fulfill Jesus' call: "If anyone desires to come after Me, let him deny himself, and take up his cross, and follow Me. " Matthew 16:24 Therefore, we must be equipped with our weapons of warfare which are not guns and knives, but rather the sword of the Spirit which is the word of God. In addition to this weapon we add righteousness, peace, salvation, and truth while practicing spiritual disciplines such as prayer fasting and meditation on the Word. Then and only then will we be able to wage a war against our true enemy who is seeking each and every day someone he can devour.

No one engaged in warfare worries themselves about the trappings of civilian life. These scriptures remind us that we must take the attitude of a soldier who willingly detaches himself from the things of civilian life. A solider has to give up many things. Some of them are bad things; pride, independence, self-will, and some of them are good things; his home, his family. Nevertheless, if a soldier is not willing to give up these things, he is not a soldier at all. The things that might entangle a soldier might be good or bad for a civilian. The soldier can't ask if something is good or bad for those who are not soldiers; he must give up anything that gets in the way of being a good soldier or serving his commanding officer. A faithful soldier does not have the right to do anything that will entangle them and make them less effective as a soldier.

On the off chance that Timothy did not carry on in hardship and in the event that he didn't set away the things that trapped him in the issues of this life, he would not be satisfying to his Commanding Officer. Jesus Christ is the leader of all heaven's armed forces. In Joshua 5:1-15, Jesus appeared to Joshua as Commander of the army of the LORD . He is our Commanding Officer, and we owe absolute allegiance to Him no matter what the situation. It is likely that Paul was chained to a soldier even as he composed this. He perceived how these officers acted, and how they complied with their bosses. Paul realized that this is the means by which a Christian must act towards their Lord.

"And also if anyone competes in athletics, he is not crowned unless he competes according to the rules. " 2 Timothy 2:5 Paul often drew upon the world of athletics for illustrations of the Christian life, mentioning track and field "If others be partakers of this power over you, are not we rather? Nevertheless we have not used this power; but suffer all things, lest we should hinder the gospel of Christ. "1 Corinthians 9:12, boxing, "I therefore so run, not as uncertainly; so fight I, not as one that beateth the air" 1 Corinthians 9:26, and wrestling, "For we wrestle not against flesh and blood, but against principalities, against powers, against the rulers of the darkness of this world, against spiritual wickedness in high places. " Ephesians 6:12. In 2 Timothy 2:5 the point is clear. An athlete can't make up the rules as he pleases; he must compete according to the rules if he wants to receive the crown.

It is conceivable that some would fall into the misconception of suspecting that we can make up our standards for our Christian life. For some individuals, their unique game plan makes a go at something like this: "I know this is sin, yet God sees, so I will simply continue going in this wrongdoing. " This goes against the behavior of a player who must compete as indicated by the standards.

Lastly we see Paul saying we must have the work ethic of the farmer. In this analogy Paul emphasized the fact that farmers are hard-working. In the same way, all who serve the Lord ought to be persistent in their work for the kingdom. Different from the fighter and the competitor, there is nothing impressive about the work an agriculturist does. It is often monotonous, exhausting, and unexciting. The country's best agriculturist really isn't a superstar. At the same time he must buckle down nonetheless. God has no spot for slothful clergymen. In the event that you won't buckle down, get out of the ministry. If you will buckle down on the off chance that you are in the spotlight, then let God change your heart.

Unlike many of us who simply want to have faith, Paul knew the value of hard work. He could say, comparing himself with the other apostles, "I labored more abundantly than they all" 1 Corinthians 15:10. Paul worked hard. He didn't just rely solely on his anointing and his calling in the ministry. Without his faithful works his ministry would have been less effective. Some individuals expect something for nothing. However, wise individuals realize that you will get out of your walk with Christ what you put into your walk with Christ. Here's an example. Many people will leave a service on Sunday and say I didn't get anything from service today. I would ask, "what did you take in?" Were you already prayed up when you went into the assembly? Were you meditating on the Word as you made your way? Was your primary reason for going to worship God or were you just in it for what you could get out of it; food for thought. If you are listening to WIIFM, what's in it for me then you probably won't get much out. Yet in the meantime, Paul realized that all the work he did was the endowment of God's grace in him: "I labored more abundantly than they all, yet not I, but the grace of God which was with me" 1 Corinthians 15:10. We too must realize that whatever we do it's all by God's grace.

When spiritual food is to be given to the congregation, the one giving the food must eat of it first. If they are not being fed from the Word of God, then they cannot really feed others. An effective pastor or teacher will get more out of the message than the audience does, and his time of preparation to teach God's word will also be a time of warm fellowship with God. Like a good farmer, any godly pastor will work hard and he will patiently await the harvest looking to the Lord for understanding.

Paul has just explained three illustrations of the Christian life a soldier, an athlete, and a farmer. Each of these three occupations needs great perseverance to succeed. The soldier who stops fighting before the battle is finished will never see victory. The athlete who stops running before the race is over will never win the race. The farmer who stops working before the harvest is complete will never see the fruit of his crops.

In these scriptures we are instructed to see the importance of perseverance, and to receive understanding from the Lord in all these things. God is faithful to give us understanding in all these things and He will be faithful to give us the grace to be strong. God gives this and we must receive it.

Paul provided a directive to Timothy with regards to the type of people needed for Kingdom assignments.

Timothy was to look for those whom he could pour apostolic doctrine and practice in to; he was to look for the quality of faithfulness. He didn't need to find smart men, popular men, strong men, easy men, perfect men, or good-looking men. Paul told him to look for faithful men. Much like when God told Samuel to look for a new King to replace Saul. When Samuel arrived at Jesse's house Jesse sent out all his son's who were aesthetically pleasing. However, none of them met God's standard. It was the son, David, who was young and perhaps not as good looking as the others, that God chose. Faithfulness and obedience is what God needs from His people.

"Remember that Jesus Christ, of the seed of David, was raised from the dead according to my gospel. " 2 Timothy 2:8 Paul did not give this admonition on the grounds that it was something Timothy may effortlessly overlook. He said it on the grounds that Timothy needed to be reminded to keep this in the cutting edge of his message. Timothy needed to keep the message that

Jesus was the Messiah of Israel, the seed of David. God's arrangement for salvation through Jesus Christ did not start when the child was conceived in Bethlehem. All of history anticipated what Jesus would do to spare us.

The incredible qualification of the validness of Jesus Christ is His resurrection from the dead. Keep in mind that Jesus was the first ever resurrected. Others, for example, Jesus' companion Lazarus, had been revived, yet only Jesus had been resurrected, raised to another realm of life, with another body, which however was much like the old, yet was still new and fitted for the glories of unceasing life. Jesus' resurrection was the confirmation that although it appeared as though He died like a common criminal, He really died as a righteous man out of love for us. Because he was the seed of David, Jesus was fully man; but, because he was raised from the dead He was also fully God. For Paul, it was essential that Timothy remember and teach the truth about who Jesus was. So must we be willing to preach and an uncompromising gospel, telling the truth in love to all those we come in contact with.

As believers the gospel belongs to us just as it did to Paul. Therefore, we should not only preach it we must believe it. It is the good news, the best news. Better than more money, more love, more status, or more stuff. The good news is about a real relationship with God through the finished work of Jesus Christ on the cross.

"Therefore I endure all things for the sake of the elect that they also may obtain the salvation which is in Christ Jesus with eternal glory. " 2 Timothy 2:10. It is easy for us to say we endure what we do in the kingdom for God. But the most reliable measure of our love for God is when we show love for His people. And that love should be about more than just leading people to Christ, but also about helping them to grow and mature in their relationship with Him.

"If we are faithless, He remains faithful. " 2 Timothy 2:13. We can't deny Jesus and we must keep our faithfulness to Him. Yet in the event that one does fall away, it does not change who God is: He stays reliable. It is a loathsome thing when individuals who name the name of Jesus show themselves unfaithful; countless people have been turned off from Jesus due to the double standards of the individuals who call themselves Christians. Be that as it may all the shiftiness of man does not invalidate the devotion of God. However the Christian can stand faithful as God enables them. Regardless of the possibility that one has been wavering, in any case they have time, as the Spirit of God calls to them even now, to turn again to the dependable God. We could be similar to the prodigal son, who woke up, saw his steadfastness, and got back to his father who had been dedicated to him the entire time.

As believers we must also keep attention on the most important things. We can't allow ourselves to be distracted by things that aren't important. "Of these things put them in remembrance, charging them before the Lord that they strive not about words to no profit but to the subverting of the hearers. " 2 Timothy 2:14. As believers our job is to keep those in the body of Christ always focused on the gospel. The congregation is continually enticed to get its center off of the message that truly matters, and is enticed to turn into a self help entertainment center, a social networking soiree, a common meeting site, or any number of different things. Yet this attraction must be opposed, and the congregation ought to never forget these things. The church must stand for the truth without becoming a den of confusion.

It is a serious matter and there is much to lose. If we take the focus off the message of God, and put the focus on human opinions and endless debates, it will result in the ruin of the hearers. The Bible says, "faith comes by hearing, and hearing by the word of God. " Romans 10:17. But when that word is skewed by individual opinions and speculation then ruin comes

Stay in your lane. Do the work God has given you to do. "Be diligent to present yourself approved to God, a worker who does not need to be ashamed, rightly dividing the word of truth. " 2 Timothy 2:15. This is probably one of the most important admonitions to us from Paul. Our goal is not to present ourselves approved to people, but to God. Our individual walks, our ministries, are not about winning a popularity contest. It's about showing our faithfulness to God. As such we should do all we can to do the best job we can for the Lord. We don't want to miss the mark and have him say that even though we presented a good façade, ultimately He does not know us because our motives were not pure. The Bible warns us that the work of each Christian will be examined at the judgment seat of Christ 2 Corinthians 5:10. Will you be ashamed when your work is examined?

Rightly dividing the word of truth should be the primary focus of all who hold themselves out as leaders in the body of Christ. We must know what it says and does not say, and how it is to be understood and how it is not to be understood. We are not to add our own opinions and ideas but instead we are to ask for divine revelation from God. It is not enough for us to merely know some Bible stories and verses and sprinkle them through our sermons Bible studies and church school lessons as illustrations. Our teaching should be a "right dividing" of the Word of God, correctly teaching others in the body. Rightly dividing can be explained in several ways when looking at the term and its use in biblical references. Rightly handle the Word of God, as one would rightly handle a sword. Plow straight with the Word of God, properly presenting the essential doctrines. Properly dissect and arrange the Word of God, as a priest would dissect and arrange an animal for sacrifice. Rightly dividing means there is such a concept as wrongly dividing; not everybody has pure motives when delivering the Word of God. We must comprehend that Biblical truth is not simply an issue surrendered over to everybody's understanding. There is a right way and a wrong way to comprehend the Bible, and a minister particularly must strive to master the right understanding. For instance, numerous people love to say when the Bible is cited, "Well, that is simply your understanding. "Their thought is, "You translate the Bible your way, I translate it my way, and someone else can translate it their way. We can never truly recognize what it implies, so don't pass judgment on me with your Bible verse. " When somebody approaches me with, "That is simply your translation," I think: "You are right that is my understanding, however it isn't simply my understanding, it is the right understanding, and we have to give careful consideration to what the Bible says when it is effectively interpreted. "this is a paramount point: The Bible does not mean simply what anybody needs it to mean. There may be a lot of people attempting to turn the Scriptures to justify their own egos and their own appetites, yet they are wrongly dividing the expressions of truth. We can't simply pick the translation that appears to be most agreeable to us, and then use it as genuine -

it must be rightly dividing the word of truth, and it must be in direct correlation with what the Bible says in the particular passage as it relates to the entire message of the Scriptures. A good example of this is when we here many in the church say "come as you are. " First of all, there is no scripture in the Bible that says that. However in Isaiah 1:18, God offers the invitation to come, though your sins are as scarlet, and He will make them white as snow. Matthew 11: 28 says, "Come unto me, all ye that labour and are heavy laden, and I will give you rest." And there are more, but contrary to the assumption made by those hearing the words come as you are over the pulpit, these verses have nothing to do with dress but everything to do with a person's soul condition. These verses and others similar to them offer each person the invitation to come to God even in their sinful nature and He will accept them and transform them. Frequently some new age ideologies take the grace of God and transform it into indecency by how you live your life is of no consequence as long as you accept Jesus. In the event that you come to Christ in an illicit relationship, they say Christ will acknowledge you as you are and purify that relationship. In the event that you come to Christ as somebody who appreciates the night life, you can continue those things, and use them to "bring others for Christ. "This may be a prevalent feel good message, yet it specifically disaffirms Scripture which obviously says that these things from our past lives ought to be abandoned and that our previous companions will think us crazy for doing so. "For the time past of our life may suffice us to have wrought the will of the Gentiles, when we walked in lasciviousness, lusts, excess of wine, revellings, banquetings, and abominable idolatries: Wherein they think it strange that ye run not with them to the same excess of riot, speaking evil of you." 1 Peter 4:3-4. Romans 13:13 orders us to "walk sincerely, or conventionally, no more taking part in the scurrilous lifestyle of the world." Galatians 5:13 says that "we are called to freedom, yet that we can't utilize freedom 'for an event to the substance,' pardoning our proceeded sins." Every believer, but leaders especially, have to work hard to seek God continuously in order to rightly divide the word of truth. They must put aside their own personal agendas, their egos, and their attitudes. And although one will never be able to know all the mysteries of the Word until Jesus' return we should still work hard at finding it.

But shun profane and idle babblings, for they will increase to more ungodliness. And their message will spread like cancer. " 2 Timothy 2:16 Hymenaeus and Philetus were two men who strayed concerning the truth, saying that the resurrection is already past. Hymenaeus is also mentioned in 1 Timothy 1:20 as a man whom Paul delivered to Satan that [he] may learn not to blaspheme. This is the only place where we hear of Philetus, and here Paul tells us of their error. They had a message full of profane and vain babblings, and apparently the message was somewhat popular, because it spread quickly. Apparently, they started out correctly, and then strayed from that correct position. It seems they were teaching that we were already in God's millennial kingdom, or that there was no resurrection to come: it had already occurred. Though the only false doctrine Paul mentioned regarding these two is that they taught that the resurrection is already past, the outcome of these erroneous teachings was to overthrow the faith of some. Fundamental error in such an important precept often leads to many more strange beliefs, until one has abandoned Jesus and His truth all together. Their teachings took the focus off of the gospel and God's Word. Their babblings were profane because they were unholy in contrast to the holiness of God's Word. These teachings were vain, because even though people liked to hear them, they did not have lasting value. The same remains true today man's opinions, man's teachings, man's stories, man's programs, are all profane and vain babblings compared to the simple Word of God. When these teachings are allowed to go forth from the pulpit even though they may sound good, spread quickly and be popular, they are like a cancer that spreads fast and captures an audience. By listening and absorbing these profane vain babblings people in the body of Christ can find their faith overthrown   which leads to an increase in ungodliness.

Many today accept and honor teachers who are way off in one area or another; and they justify it by saying, "I eat the meat and spit out the bones. " This kind of thinking will certainly overthrow the faith of some, because some will certainly choke to spiritual death on the bones you say you spit out.

"Nevertheless the solid foundation of God stands, having this seal: The Lord knows those who are His, and, Let everyone who names the name of Christ depart from iniquity." 2 Timothy 2:19 One might think that in this passage Paul was under attack. It may even sound like he might not stand against the rising tide of trickery and wickedness. But here, he makes it clear, both to himself and to us that the kingdom of God cannot be shaken. Though men like Hymenaeus and Philetus made dangerous attacks against the church and their message spread like cancer, and even though the faith of some might be overthrown, nevertheless, the solid foundation of God stands. God has a plan, God has a purpose, God has a strategy, and it is not going to fail. It does not matter how many fall away, how many reject the truth, how many go out on their own after these scandalous mistruths have been put forth; nevertheless, the solid foundation of God stands.

Our identification with the risen and enthroned Lord Jesus helps us to understand that we can put to death the things in our life that are contrary to our identity with Jesus. Fornication, uncleanness, passion and evil desire, each of these terms refers to sexual sins. Covetousness is simple, but insidious greed, nothing less than idolatry. Each of these is part of the way the world lives and not the way Jesus lives. There is no way that Jesus would walk in any of these sins, so if we identify with Him, we won't walk in them either. Every Christian is faced with a question: "Who will I identify with, the world or with Jesus?"

These wrongdoings welcome the rage of God. And since the world cherishes this sort of evil lifestyle, they don't come in lowliness to Jesus. As they proceed in these wrongdoings, it adds to their judgment. One transgression is sufficient to send anybody to damnation however there are more noteworthy levels of judgment "Woe unto you, scribes and Pharisees, hypocrites! for ye devour widows' houses, and for a pretence make long prayer: therefore ye shall receive the greater damnation. " Matthew 23:14. To a limited extent, the rage of God comes as God permits men to proceed in corrupt, and consequently self-destructive, conduct. As in the following passage of scripture, "Wherefore God also gave them up to uncleanness through the lusts of their own hearts, to dishonour their own bodies between themselves: Who changed the truth of God into a lie, and worshipped and served the creature more than the Creator, who is blessed forever. Amen. For this cause God gave them up unto vile affections: for even their women did change the natural use into that which is against nature: And likewise also the men, leaving the natural use of the woman, burned in their lust one toward another; men with men working that which is unseemly, and receiving in themselves that recompence of their error which was meet. And even as they did not like to retain God in their knowledge, God gave them over to a reprobate mind, to do those things which are not convenient; Being filled with all unrighteousness, fornication, wickedness, covetousness, maliciousness; full of envy, murder, debate, deceit, malignity; whisperers, Backbiters, haters of God, despiteful, proud, boasters, inventors of evil things, disobedient to parents, Without understanding, covenant breakers, without natural affection, implacable, unmerciful: Who knowing the judgment of God, that they which commit such things are worthy of death, not only do the same, but have pleasure in them that do them. " Romans 1:24-32.

These wrongdoings are the stain of a world in resistance to God, yet they are in reality the previous existence experienced by many Christians. Basically put, the Christian ought not to live like the children of disobedience. A genuine Christian can't be agreeable with sustained sin. Paul says that Christians once lived in these transgressions. It is conceivable, however deplorable, that these transgressions might every so often come up in a Christian's life, yet they should not be a Christian's walk, or their way of living.

"But now you yourselves are to put off all these: anger, wrath, malice, blasphemy, filthy language out of your mouth. Do not lie to one another, since you have put off the old man with his deeds" Colossians 3:8. The wrongdoings Paul next records are viewed by a lot of people as "little" sins that Christians may neglect with little to no consequence. Paul provokes us to put off the old man in every part of our lives, anger, wrath, malice, blasphemy, filthy language out of your mouth. Each of these transgressions is fundamentally committed by what we say. At the point when Paul calls the believer to a deeper obedience, he let us us know that we must consistently seek to harness our tongue.

The more notorious sins of Colossians 3:5 are easily seen as incompatible with the nature of Jesus. But these "lesser" sins are also incompatible, so put off these sins as well. "Mortify therefore your members which are upon the earth; fornication, uncleanness, inordinate affection, evil concupiscence, and covetousness, which is idolatry: For which things' sake the wrath of God cometh on the children of disobedience: In the which ye also walked some time, when ye lived in them. But now ye also put off all these; anger, wrath, malice, blasphemy, filthy communication out of your mouth. Lie not one to another, seeing that ye have put off the old man with his deeds"

In this passage of scripture Colossians 3:5-9, Paul

demonstrated two important necessities in Christian living: sexual ethical quality in conjunction with a right disposition towards material things, and basic getting along in love with each other. It is simple for a Christian group to bargain one for the other, however Paul, by impulse of the Holy Spirit, demanded that they both have a high place in Christian practice. You have put off the old man with his deeds implies that in Jesus Christ, those who exemplify godliness are distinctive individuals. "Therefore, as we put off the old man, we must put on the new man and have put on the new man who is renewed in knowledge according to the image of Him who created him, where there is neither Greek nor Jew, circumcised nor uncircumcised, barbarian, Scythian, slave nor free, but Christ is all and in all. " Colossians 3:11 Put on the new man: This was a phrase commonly used for changing a set of clothes. We can almost picture a person taking off the old and putting on the new man in Jesus.

The new man is part of a family, which favors no

race, nationality, class, culture or ethnicity. It only favors Jesus, because in this new family, Christ is all and in all. This work of the new creation not only deals with the old man and gives us the new man patterned after Jesus Christ; it also breaks down the barriers that separate people in society. Among new creation people it does not matter if one is Greek or Jew or circumcised or uncircumcised or a Scythian or a slave or a free man. All those barriers are broken down. All of these barriers existed in the ancient Roman world; and the power of God through the Gospel of Jesus Christ broke them all down. Especially powerful was the barrier between slave and free, but Christianity changed that.

"Therefore, as the elect of God, holy and beloved, put on tender mercies, kindness, humility, meekness, longsuffering; bearing with one another, and forgiving one another, If anyone has a complaint against another; even as Christ forgave you, so you also must do. But above all these things put on love, which is the bond of perfection. And let the peace of God rule in your hearts, to which also you were called in one body; and be thankful. Let the word of Christ dwell in you richly in all wisdom, teaching and admonishing one another in psalms and hymns and spiritual songs, singing with grace in your hearts to the Lord. And whatever you do in word or deed, do all in the name of the Lord Jesus, giving thanks to God the Father through Him. " Colossians 3:12-13 NKJV. The new man is elect of God. This means that God has chosen the Christian, and chosen him to be something special in His plan. Tender mercies, kindness, humility, each one of these qualities mentioned in this passage express themselves in relationships. A significant measure of our Christian life is found simply in how we treat people and the quality of our relationships with them. The glue that holds all of these together is unconditional love.

"Forbearing one another, and forgiving one another, if any man have a quarrel against any: even as Christ forgave you, so also do ye. " Colossians 3:13 We are advised to live overlooking each other's faults and offenses, after the example of Jesus' absolution towards us. Understanding the way Jesus forgave us will unfailingly make us more liberal with pardoning others. When we consider the stunning debt Jesus overlooked for us, and the relative diminutiveness of the obligations others have to us, it is pure unadulterated thoughtlessness for us to not forgive them as in the parable Jesus spoke in Matthew 18:21-35. "Then came Peter to him, and said, Lord, how oft shall my brother sin against me, and I forgive him? till seven times? Jesus saith unto him, I say not unto thee, Until seven times: but, Until seventy times seven. Therefore is the kingdom of heaven likened unto a certain king, which would take account of his servants. And when he had begun to reckon, one was brought unto him, which owed him ten thousand talents. But forasmuch as he had not to pay, his lord commanded him to be sold, and his wife, and children, and all that he had, and payment to be made."

At the point when one considers how Christ forgave you it ought to make us a great deal more liberal with forgiving one another. God keeps down His outrage quite a while when we sin against Him even though we woefully provoke Him. God connects with terrible individuals to bring forgiveness to them; the tendency of men is to forget about forgiveness if the responsible individual is one of bad character. God makes the first move towards us in forgiveness; the inclination of men is to only forgive if the guilty person longs for absolution and makes the first move. God forgives over and over again realizing that we will sin once more. It is the propensity of men to overlook offense just if the offending party guarantees to never do the wrong again. God's absolution is so absolute and wonderful that He allows for the offender to return to the body of Christ with no condemnation. In the pattern of man, even when forgiveness is offered, our response is to not lift the guilty party to a position of high status or leadership. God bore all the punishment for the wrong we did against Him. In the practice of man, when he is wronged, he won't pardon unless the guilty party consents to shoulder all the punishment for the wrong done. God continues reaching out to man for compromise even when man rejects Him over and over. In the custom of men, one won't keep on offering compromise in the event that it is rejected once. God obliges no trial period to get His forgiveness; in the tradition of men, one won't restore a guilty party without a time of probation. God's pardoning offers complete restoration and honor; in the minds of men, we feel we ought to be complimented when we endure the individuals who sin against us. Having forgiven, God puts His trust in us and welcomes us again to work with Him as co-laborers. In the limited understanding of men, one won't believe somebody who has previously wronged them.

Suppose that someone had grievously offended any one of you, and that he asked your forgiveness, do you not think that you would probably say to him, 'Well, yes, I forgive you; but I - I - I - cannot forget it'? Well, bless the Lord that when God forgives us He casts our transgressions into the sea of forgetfulness; food for thought.

If there is ever to be unity in the body of Christ, unconditional love will have to be its predecessor. "Above all these things put on love, which is the bond of perfection" Love is the summary of all the things described in this passage. Love perfectly fulfills what God requires of us in relationships. "Put on therefore, as the elect of God, holy and beloved, bowels of mercies, kindness, humbleness of mind, meekness, longsuffering; Forbearing one another, and forgiving one another, if any man have a quarrel against any: even as Christ forgave you, so also do you. " Colossians 3:12-13

The new man walks in the word of God and in worship with other believers because he allows the word of Christ to actively live in him and he uses that word to walk in all wisdom, teaching and admonishing others in psalms and hymns and spiritual songs as is spoken of in the text.

The new man lives his life, all his life, for Jesus. He will only seek to do the things that he may do in the name of the Lord Jesus, and he will persevere in the difficulty of doing such things, knowing that he is doing them in the name of the Lord Jesus.

God gives those whose part is to equip others for their parts. The result is growth, maturity and solidarity, on the off chance that we permit the outcome to come about as God proposed. Some Christian development and education originates from companions; a few originates from individuals in the congregation who have the particular work of showing and demonstrating the Christian life. Individuals who segregate themselves are passing up a major opportunity to experience this part of the faith.

There is much work to be done. More Bible studies, trainings in evangelism, and classes for new believers should be offered by local ministry leaders in an attempt to edify and equip the body for true discipleship.

When we fellowship one with another it creates relationships among us and other Christians. We all need to offer and to accept cooperation. We all need to give and get love. Our week after week gatherings exhibit that partnership is essential to us. Association implies a great deal more than conversing with one another about games, gossip and news. It means sharing testimonies about our lives, imparting our feelings and emotions, bearing one another's troubles, empowering each other and helping the individuals who have need.

Most individuals make a facade to conceal their needs from others. In the event that we are truly going to help each other, we have to draw near enough to each other to see behind the dividers that have been raised to shroud the reality that is our lives. It implies that we need to let our own dividers tumble down a bit so others can see our needs. Little gatherings are a decent place in which to do this. We get to know individuals somewhat better and feel a little more secure with them. Frequently, they are solid in the area in which we are weak, and we are solid where they are frail. So by supporting each other, we both get to be stronger. Indeed the messenger Paul, despite the fact that he was a Goliath in the faith, he felt that he could be reinforced in confidence by other Christians. "That is, that I may be comforted together with you by the mutual faith both of you and me. " Romans 1:12.

In antiquated times, individuals didn't move around as frequently. Groups were more easily created in which individuals knew one another. At the same time in industrialized social orders today, individuals frequently don't have a clue about their neighbors. Individuals are frequently cut off from families and companions. In this way, those in the body of Christ ought to do all that they can to structure groups that address the individual needs of the people in their "village." Their spiritual needs as well as their physical. After all it has been said,

"People don't care how much you know until they know how much you care."

This will require some serious energy, yes. It truly requires significant investment to satisfy our Christian obligations. It requires some serious energy to serve others. It even requires some serious energy to discover what sorts of administration they require. However if we have acknowledged Jesus as our Lord, our time is not our own. Jesus Christ makes requests on our lives. He requests all out duty, not a fake Christianity.

"As we have opportunity, let us do good to all people, especially to those who belong to the family of believers" Galatians 6:10. Far too often because of the spirit of competition and the spirit of elitism we find ourselves far away from the mandate set forth in this scripture. God has placed each of us in the body "for the common good" 1 Corinthians 12:7. My favorite scripture says God can do some big things according to what He has already gifted us to do. Each of us has abilities that can help others. We simply need to find out what those gifts and talents are and then operate in them. In addition we need to seek out places where we can best utilize those gifts for the edification of the body. Everyone will not be receptive to your gifts for a variety of reasons; jealousy, envy, greed, etc. Therefore, we must be discerning and know when to move on to the place God has ordained us to be. And you will know when you are there because the people will be open to what you have to offer. As members of the body of Christ we should serve the world in word, as well as in deeds that correspond with those words. Scripture reminds us we should be doers and not just hearers of the Word. Our talk should be carried forth in our walk. God did not simply talk — he made a move. Activities can exhibit the adoration of God working in our hearts, as we help poor people, as we offer solace to the debilitated, as we help victimized people understand their lives. It is the people who need commonsense help who are frequently the most receptive to the gospel message.

Killing Religion

In various ways doing benevolent acts may be seen as supporting the gospel. It could be seen as a strategy for supporting evangelism. Yet some benevolent acts should be finished with no stipulations, no desire of accepting something in return. We serve basically on the grounds that God has given us gifts and talents and has opened our eyes to see a need. Jesus sought after and supported various people without any sudden solicitation for them to transform into his followers. He did it fundamentally in light of the fact that it was something that had to be carried out, and he saw a need that He could fill.

"Go into all the world and preach the gospel," Jesus commands us. Honestly, we need a lot of improvement in this area. We have been too conditioned to keep our faith to ourselves. Of course, people cannot be converted unless the Father is calling them, but that fact does not mean that we should not preach the gospel!

Getting to be viable propelling witnesses of the

166

gospel message will necessitate a social change inside the body of Christ. We can no longer afford to kick back and depend on others to do it for us. Evangelism is the obligation of every single kingdom citizen. Whether we are leaders or not not we are all ministers for Christ and we ought to have as our primary reason responsibility the discipleship of men and women.

Evangelism needs an individual face. At the point when God needed to make an impression on individuals, he utilized individuals to do it. He sent his Son, God in human form, to lecture. Today he sends His followers, His modern day disciples, His children, people in whom the Spirit is residing, to teach the message. We have to be dynamic, eager and anxious to impart the truth of God's gospel. We should be eager about spreading the good news with an energy that conveys something dynamic about Christianity to our neighbors. Do they even realize that we are Christians? Does it seem as though we are excited to be Christians? We are developing and growing in this, however we require more development.

I encourage every person who sees themselves as kingdom minded to offer thought to how we may each be Christian witnesses to those around us. I urge each believer to comply with the order to be ready to give an account. I urge each person to pay particular attention to evangelism, and then apply what you know to win souls. We can all learn together and drive each other to benevolent acts. It does not take a multitude; just a few willing kingdom builders sold out for the cause of making disciples of men and women.

It would not be unheard of for members of a congregation to learn faster than its ministers, pastors or leaders. In the event that that is the situation then the ministry leaders can glean from those in the body. God has gifted each of us differently. He has blessed us with a diversity of talents and each one is just as important as the other. To some of our parts, he has given a blessing for evangelism that needs to be stirred up and cultivated. In case the clergyman can't equip this believer for this sort of administration, the clergyman ought to encourage the saint to learn, execute, and offer representations to others, so that the whole church may grow and develop. The congregation of believers is God's hands, mouth and feet in this world. 1 Corinthians 12:12-27. We should be doing the things Christ would do if He were here.

Epilogue

"Behold I will do a new thing…" Isaiah 43:19

God is doing a new thing. He is re-making His actual Church, the true Church. He is set to do away with these religious practices and customs that have compromised the house of worships power. I am referring to the Church; the one that makes it conceivable for individuals who truly have faith in Him to see His purpose fulfilled in their lives. His purpose is to see all of us transformed into the image of Christ. "For whom he did foreknow, he also did predestinate to be conformed to the image of his Son, that he might be the firstborn among many brethren." Romans 8:29. The Father wants to strip away everything in us that does not look like Jesus through the indwelling of the Holy Spirit.

Our diluted idea of church has us preaching a "Barney the purple dinosaur message" I love you, you love me we're a happy family; when nothing could be further from reality. We speak a gospel that makes individuals feel great not just with themselves but with God. We need to tell individuals any way the wind blows it is alright because we want to encourage their continued attendance. Do what you need to do to make yourself happy. Simply come to church on Sunday and remember to leave your tithes and offering in the collection plate. Don't stress; God will reach out to you where you are. No progression needed. Overlook atonement, we should just be happy. There is more than one approach to God. I will see you in heaven. Church service today is intended to give individuals what they need, what God requires is unimportant. Not all together unexpected since it is man" who is charge instead of God. Understanding the genuine church and not religion obliges us to take an insightful look at the scriptures on the grounds that in opposition to what you may read in Church history books of different denominations, these denominations have not cornered the market on Christendom.

No the first church consisted of Jesus and His 12 disciples meeting in houses, gardens, on mountaintops, and at seaside. Wherever Jesus was that is where the church was. Jesus was forming their understanding of what church was supposed to be and established a pattern for the next generation of churches.

Let me describe to you what one of these gatherings in this first congregation must have looked like. When it was the ideal time for the gathering everybody put on their Sunday go to meeting clothes, snatched a hymnbook and an enormous, fat Bible to put under their arm. At that point they all went down to the building with the sign out front that said "First Church". The marquee had the sermon theme for the day: "How to Boost Your Self Esteem", and the name of the class that would meet that evening, "Divorce Recovery at 6 PM". Everybody filed in, sat down on their favorite pew, all eyes on the preacher, waiting for the minister of music to play the first chord. They sang three praise and worship numbers, two fast and one slow, recited from memory the Apostles Creed or some other litany they had learned, sang a congregational hymn, passed the offering plate and listened to a special selection from the choir. At that point Jesus, looking radiant in a sparkling, blue, handmade robe, with a truly incredible 18 carat gold cross tucked in neatly to one side, took the podium and conveyed a soothing, to some degree entertaining, thirty-minute sermon. Everybody liked what they had heard and complimented Jesus on what a wonderful work He had finished, and after that they all headed off to lunch. Furthermore Jesus was glad that nobody was uncomfortable with what He had said and felt beyond any doubt that a large portion of them might return one week from now. What's more in the fulfillment of a job well done, He soon overlooked the entire thing and started to contemplate something truly imperative, the Sunday afternoon football game. That is about the gist of it right? No?

Not convinced? Well, you should not be. The first church looked nothing like what we see today. In fact, Matthew 5:1 to 8:1 gives us a good idea of what the services were like in Jesus' day. The church edifice was small but the people were there in great numbers. They were so enthralled by what they were hearing they stayed through the entire message even though it was quite long. Subsequently Jesus held several "meetings" with His followers. "And when Jesus was entered into Capernaum, there came unto him a centurion, beseeching him, And saying, Lord, my servant lieth at home sick of the palsy, grievously tormented. And Jesus saith unto him, I will come and heal him. The centurion answered and said, Lord, I am not worthy that thou shouldest come under my roof: but speak the word only, and my servant shall be healed. For I am a man under authority, having soldiers under me: and I say to this man, Go, and he goeth; and to another, Come, and he cometh; and to my servant, Do this, and he doeth it. When Jesus heard it, he marveled, and said to them that followed, Verily I say unto you, I have not found so great faith, no, not in Israel. And I say unto you, That many shall come from the east and west, and shall sit down with Abraham, and Isaac, and Jacob, in the kingdom of heaven. But the children of the kingdom shall be cast out into outer darkness: there shall be weeping and gnashing of teeth. And Jesus said unto the centurion, Go thy way; and as thou hast believed, so be it done unto thee. And his servant was healed in the selfsame hour." Matthew 8:5-13 "And when Jesus was come into Peter's house, he saw his wife's mother laid, and sick of a fever. And he touched her hand, and the fever left her: and she arose, and ministered unto them. When the even was come, they brought unto him many that were possessed with devils: and he cast out the spirits with his word, and healed all that were sick: That it might be fulfilled which was spoken by Esaias the prophet, saying, Himself took our infirmities, and bare our sicknesses." Matthew 8:14-17

The first church was living with Jesus. It's actually really simple. Every church, even the twenty first century church should have as its ultimate goal the equipping of every believer to walk with Jesus. The church should be promoting that every believer have a closer walk with Jesus

The straightforward truth is that congregations should be the help, the supportive network for believers in their consistent, continuous association with Jesus. It should help them in their steady, candidly transparent, submissive, dutiful, all around beneficial, converting, reestablishing, Holy Spirit-headed, love relationship with the Savior; and assuming that you are willing to be transformed into the image of Christ, that is the lifestyle that is needed. How else would you be able to be changed into something you have not encountered and submitted yourself to? When you read your Bible outside of the overarching religious predisposition and deception you will understand that this is salvation, plain and simple. The Bible does not portray salvation as something that dependent upon something you have done having your name on the church roles, baptism, affirmation classes, and so forth. Salvation is a certainty that is dependent upon what you are completing today. It is dependent upon the firm commitment to a nonstop association with God that requires your compliance to His will and reason. It obliges change yours, not His. It also requires a sacrifice, some suffering, and yes, a few trials. But the good news is we are promised the victory. I mean really think about it how are you going to have a victory if there is never a battle? If you only read the red letters in the Gospel accounts, you will see that Jesus never depicts salvation as something that is fast and simple just religious impersonators utilizing segregated verses do that. Rather, He introduces it as something that is challenging, something that requires perseverance and something that just a few will accomplish.

Salvation is not dependent upon what you think about God, Jesus made that impeccably clear. It's not an intelligent activity; it is a lifestyle. It is existing with Jesus. The congregation is an assembly of individuals living with Jesus, offering their encounters to each one in turn, as they live with Him. A group of followers experiencing change together, submitting to His will and intention, being transformed into a picture of Christ, as they are saved. Salvation is a continuous process. "And he said to them all, If any man will come after me, let him deny himself, and take up his cross daily, and follow me. For whosoever will save his life shall lose it: but whosoever will lose his life for my sake, the same shall save it." Luke 9:23-24; "Wherefore, my beloved, as ye have always obeyed, not as in my presence only, but now much more in my absence, work out your own salvation with fear and trembling. For it is God which worketh in you both to will and to do of his good pleasure." Philippians. 2:12-13 I am astounded at the amount of churches today who make a case for being "New Testament", yet have nothing whatsoever that would even remotely connect them to the New Testament church we find in scripture. Most are simply regular houses of worship searching for new and inventive approaches to lure more individuals, while attempting to decipher how you can adequately divert them while they are there, so they will give their stamp of approval to the entire arrangement and return the following week. In the meantime, the "church folk" slip something religious into the mix, so the people think they had some gushy, nostalgic experience with God.

You should not have to learn this information from a book. Nor should you have to learn it only from a sermon delivered on a Sunday morning. You should submit yourself to the Spirit of God living inside you and allow

Him to pour into you and reveal to you the things of God. However, there is a lot of deception in the throes of religion today, and in the absence of truth, it is necessary to offer a roadmap for those interested in finding the truth for themselves.

So let us now take a look at what the book of Ephesians can share with us can that can help us restore our churches to their proper position as we enter into the end times. "With all lowliness and gentleness, with long-suffering, bearing with one another in love, endeavoring to keep the unity of the Spirit in the bond of peace. There is one body and one Spirit, just as you were called in one hope of your calling; one Lord, one faith, one baptism; one God and Father of all, who is above all, and through all, and in you all. " Ephesians 4:1-6

It is clear in these writings of Paul that God freely by his grace has already done more than enough for us all. In fact, the first three chapters spell this out for us very plainly. Therefore our understanding how much

God did for us is pivotal to our ability to establish a foundation for our Christian walk. We must walk worthy not so that God will love us but because He loves us. We are His and He has proven it time and time again by His willingness to bless us even in spite of ourselves. Because we cannot earn His grace, mercy, or blessings our service to Him should be born out of our gratitude for what He has already done and what He will do in the future.

Our own agendas and our own desires become a thing of the past when we walk a walk of holiness and gentleness. Unlike the connotation the word lowliness generally brings, it simply means that we can be happy and content when we are not in control or steering things our way. We can humble ourselves before an almighty God and allow Him to be in control of our lives.

Longsuffering, and bearing with one another is necessary. Inevitably offense will occur in the body of Christ just as it does in the world. In fact,, the Bible reminds us of this very thing. However Ephesians tells us that we are to be longsuffering and bear with one another. Why because not doing so would work against God's ultimate purpose of bringing unity to the body of Christ.

This reminds me of David in 2 Samuel the second and third chapters. In these two books we see the division of the Israelite people. Saul and his sons were killed by the Philistines. David was in the process of consolidating Israel under his leadership. King Saul's loss to the Philistines in the battle that cost him and his sons their lives was costly to Israel as a nation. Not only did Israel lose their king, but they also lost territory and numerous battle-hardened, experienced warriors. Israel, which was not in wonderful condition under Saul's leadership, was now weakened further, vulnerable, and divided. The Philistines must have rejoiced at the situation because circumstances surely favored them.

David and his forces, with God's approval, went to the area of Hebron where the people made him king of Judah. Abner, the commander of King Saul's army, made

Saul's son, Ish-bosheth King over what was left of Israel excluding Judah. Abner, a relative of dead King Saul, was the man of power in Israel. Ish-bosheth was King Saul's son and the symbol of royal presence.

The end result, there was a long period of tension and civil war among the Israelites. In this period, David sought to consolidate Israel as a single nation. In this civil war, the forces of Saul's family steadily grew weaker and David's forces steadily grew stronger.

While there were numerous battles in that long civil war conflict, the there was one key battle that stands out as the opportunity for David to bear with his brother. David's sister, Zeruiah, had three sons: Joab, Abishai, and Asahel. These three men figured prominently in David's army. Joab was the commander over David's forces. The other two brothers were elite warriors in David's army. They were capable of both great loyalty and thoughtless acts.

In this battle, the two forces were on opposite sides

of the pool of Gibeon. Much like the occasions that involved Goliath's challenges to Israel's army, each side decided it served no purpose to have a huge battle with lots of deaths. Each side decided to have twenty-four less experienced warriors, twelve men from each side; engage in battle to provide an indication of which group was strongest. Nothing was settled because the twenty-four men killed each other. When that occurred, a full battle broke out. Eventually the forces representing Saul's family fled from David's forces.

In the process of the battle, Asahel, Joab's youngest brother, decided that he would pursue and kill Abner. Asahel was quite fast, and Abner was quite experienced. Abner, confident that he could kill Asahel, did not wish to do so. He either feared or respected Joab, Asahel's brother. Abner tried twice to convince Asahel to discontinue his pursuit. When Asahel refused, Abner killed him with the back of his spear--an indication of how close to Abner Asahel was. Asahel's death made this civil war a matter of personal vendetta for Joab. Abner killed Joab's youngest brother, so Joab as an avenger of blood had the right to kill Abner if he could.

The battle continued until evening. Finally Abner convinced Joab to call a truce. Both sides acknowledged it was not appropriate for Israelites to pursue and kill Israelites. Each side counted their losses and made lengthy journeys back home.

The civil war took a decided turn in David's favor when Ish-bosheth insulted Abner. Abner reacted to the insult by swearing he would make David King of Israel. From that time forward Ish-bosheth was afraid of Abner. He knew Abner controlled the power, and he knew Abner made him King.

Abner sent messengers to David affirming that he could make David King of Israel. He asked David to make a covenant with him. David immediately accepted the opportunity with one condition: his first wife Michal, King Saul's daughter, would be returned to David.

Killing Religion

Michal was returned to David. Abner began the process of convincing Israel to turn to David for leadership. Finally, Abner came with 20 men to David in Hebron. David honored Abner with a feast. The agreement for David to become King of all Israel was confirmed. Abner left in peace with David's blessing.

Joab returned from a raid after Abner departed. When he learned that Abner was at Hebron, he criticized David. "He came to deceive you! He came to learn how to attack you!"

Unknown to David, Joab sent messengers to catch up with Abner and have him return to Sirah. At Sirah, as Abner thought all was well, Joab killed him to avenge the death of his brother. When David heard what Joab did, he was both grieved and frustrated. He wanted everyone to know he had nothing to do with Abner's death. In fact, he placed a curse on Joab and his descendants; commanded the people to mourn Abner's death; expressed his personal grief in a tribute to Abner; and

186

refused to eat during the day of Abner's burial.

The people were pleased with David's proper reaction to Abner's death. They understood that Abner's death had nothing to do with David's desire.

David acted as a man of character in Abner's death. He sought to do something extremely difficult in a time of civil war, heal a nation. Joab's act would have made that healing impossible had not David been a man of character and humility. Again, David placed an extremely difficult situation in God's hands -- "May the Lord repay the evildoer according to his evil. " Joab acted in hate to pacify his desire for personal vengeance. David acted in respect in the desire to heal a nation bearing with his brother and showing longsuffering in the process.

This humble, forgiving attitude towards each other creates something quite different from the structural or denominational unity we cater to. It creates a spiritual unity. We don't have to create it but we are responsible for keeping it. God never commands us to create unity among believers. He has created it by His Spirit; our duty is to recognize it and keep it. This is a spiritual unity, not necessarily a structural or denominational unity. Spiritual tyranny and ecclesiastical arrangements are not elements associated with this type of unity. Instead they often become misdirected efforts that morph into huge spiritual corporations, strongholds of tyranny and places of abuse that are reduced to mere enrollment on a register instead of a union with Christ and each other. We need unity in the truth of God through the Spirit of God. There is no division where the true spirit of love exists.

Spiritual Leadership in the church was originally orchestrated by Jesus Himself. It had purpose. "And He Himself gave some to be apostles, some prophets, some evangelists, and some pastors and teachers, for the equipping of the saints for the work of ministry, for the edifying of the body of Christ," 2. Ephesians 4:11-12

Contrary to the belief that is present in the church today these leadership roles are divine in nature as opposed to human invention. In scripture Paul describes four offices, not five, as in the commonly yet inaccurately termed "five-fold" ministry. The first of these was Apostles, who are special ambassadors of God's work. They were used to provide a foundation as described in Ephesians 2:20. The second office is that of Prophets, who speak forth words from God in total consistency with the foundation of the Old and New Testaments. Sometimes they speak in a predictive sense, but not necessarily so, and they are always subject to the discernment and judgment of the church leadership as in 1 Corinthians 14:29. The third office is the Evangelist, who is specifically gifted to preach the good news of salvation in Jesus Christ. Lastly there are Pastors and teachers, or, pastor-teachers; the ancient Greek clearly describes one office with two descriptive titles, who shepherd the flock of God primarily though not exclusively through teaching the Word of God. These gifts are given at the discretion of

Jesus, working through the Holy Spirit as in 1 Corinthians 12:11. The importance of having all four in operations in any church body is up to Jesus who appoints the offices. The job of responsible church leadership is to not hinder or prevent such ministry, but never to "promote it into existence." The purpose of these gifts of leadership is that God's people might be equipped for the work of ministry or service, so that the body of Christ would be built up, expanded, and strengthened. You see God's people do the real work of ministry. True leaders are servant leaders who build up and empower others to lead, and serve according to the grace God has given them.

We need not look anywhere else other than the Word of God to understand the outcome He is seeking through the work of leadership. "Till we all come to the unity of the faith and of the knowledge of the Son of God, to a perfect man, to the measure of the stature of the fullness of Christ; that we should no longer be children, tossed to and fro and carried about with every wind of doctrine, by the trickery of men, in the cunning craftiness of deceitful plotting, but, speaking the truth in love, may grow up in all things into Him who is the head; Christ; from whom the whole body, joined and knit together by what every joint supplies, according to the effective working by which every part does its share, causes growth of the body for the edifying of itself in love. " Ephesians 4:13-16 Equipped saints and leadership should work together to unify the body of Christ. This is consistent with both the ultimate purpose of God Ephesians 1:10 and the mystery of God revealed through Paul Ephesians 3:6. Believers can grow spiritually and experience a greater intimacy with God when those equipped by effective leadership that their rightful position. Furthermore I firmly believe that the "growing old" spoken of in Proverbs with reference to training up children as well as the "older" men and "older" women of Titus 2 is in direct reference to spiritual maturity as opposed to chronological age; such as with

Samuel who was deemed a prophet at an early age of about no more than 17 or Daniel who was about 14 or 15. Each of these men was integral to the Kingdom because of their spiritual maturity. "We should no longer be children, tossed to and fro and carried about with every wind of doctrine" Ephesians 2:20. "Be sober be vigilant; because your adversary the devil, as a roaring lion, walketh about, seeing whom he may devour. " 1 Peter 5:8. When we fail to reach spiritual maturity we leave ourselves as open prey for our adversary the devil that is full of deception, and trickery just waiting to devour us. Religion's creation of denominationalism has produced churches beholden only to themselves and not necessarily to the will of God for the church. Churches may be united in their traditions but there is no real life giving unity that can only be experienced when God through the Holy Spirit is allowed to lead. The Body of Christ will only have matured when each member of the body is effectively working in a coordinated effort to bring about the kingdom of God here on earth. That is why the unity of Israel was so important to David in 2 Samuel. He knew that this kind of unity would bring about growth in numbers and in strength. The Body of Christ is a pyramid where the leadership or the pastor is on the top. Nor is it an entity full of blinded people who need to be passively led to where they need to go. God wants everyone in the body to be equipped enough to do their share.

In other words if we want to effectively usher in the kingdom of God , the church of God, the way it was originally intended, we must not look like the world looks. Nor must we look like others within the body. Instead, we must look more like Christ. "This I say, therefore, and testify in the Lord, that you should no longer walk as the rest of the Gentiles walk, in the futility of their mind, having their understanding darkened, being alienated from the life of God, because of the ignorance that is in them, because of the blindness of their heart; who, being past feeling, have given themselves over to lewdness, to work all uncleanness with greediness. " Ephesians 4:17-19.

Bound by our religious traditions and insensitivity to any real spirituality along with our constant need to gain the world's respect or approval, we now live in the futility of the world's reasoning. We have left ourselves closed to the leading of the Holy Spirit that would open us up and allow us to be turned around and pointed in the right direction.

So how do we keep ourselves from looking like the world, by putting on the new man? "But you have not so learned Christ, if indeed you have heard Him and have been taught by Him, as the truth is in Jesus: that you put off, concerning your former conduct, the old man which grows corrupt according to the deceitful lusts, and be renewed in the spirit of your mind, and that you put on the new man which was created according to God, in true righteousness and holiness. " 2. Ephesians 4:20-24

My point of view is this, a homeless homeless

jobless person could come to you. Your response as a believer would hopefully be to offer them aid. Perhaps a place to stay and a hot meal. Ultimately, you would offer them some new clothes. You would lean towards helping them understand how a new look, a new wardrobe could bring about an entirely new understanding, a different perspective. Just like putting on new clothes will change the way you think about yourself and see yourself, putting on an alternate mentality will begin to change your disposition. This implies that we can feel like the new man even before we put on the new man. We must make a complete and total break from our

past to carry on with another life in Jesus. We don't simply include Jesus in our plans and agendas. Rather we

turn our backs and permit the old life to pass away while we get to be restored in our personalities and submit ourselves wholly to the new life we've discovered. It is more than just having a carnal intellectual understanding of who God is. It is about understanding Him. We should not simply learn of Him we must learn Him. This implies a living, breathing growing knowledge of Jesus. This is what will ultimately keep us from the sort of corrupt conduct Paul talks about. Simply thinking about Jesus is not enough to keep us holy. The new man is the "new creation" as spoken of in 2 Corinthians 5:17. is the individual made as indicated by the picture of Jesus Christ and naturally upright and sacred. It is as opposed to the old man, who is the individual inherited from Adam and naturally defies God. It is the person created according to the image of Jesus Christ and instinctively righteous and holy. It is in contrast to the old man, who is the person inherited from Adam and instinctively rebels against God.

So, how do we conduct ourselves as the new man? "Therefore, putting away lying, "Let each one of you speak truth with his neighbor," for we are members of one another. "Be angry, and do not sin": do not let the sun go down on your wrath, nor give place to the devil. Let him who stole steal no longer, but rather let him labor, working with his hands what is good, that he may have something to give him who has need. Let no corrupt word proceed out of your mouth, but what is good for necessary edification, that it may impart grace to the hearers. And do not grieve the Holy Spirit of God, by whom you were sealed for the day of redemption. Let all bitterness, wrath, anger, clamor, and evil speaking be put away from you, with all malice. And be kind to one another, tenderhearted, forgiving one another, just as God in Christ forgave you. " Ephesians 4:20-24 Truth telling, especially truth telling in love, is essential to the success of the body. Therefore, the new man tells the truth. Because we are all members of the same body, lying can only serve to hurt the body as a whole.

Controlling ones emotions and bringing them into submission, particularly anger, is a tell tale sign that the new man is in control. The new man may get angry, but he does not sin. The new man knows how to let go of his wrath, thus denying the enemy a foothold in which he can create strongholds of un-forgiveness and bitterness; when the new man's emotions are stirred, the new man deals with them in a way that glorifies God. The new man seeks to show the same kindness, tender heartedness and forgiveness to others that God shows him because he recognizes the devil's work is to accuse and divide the family of God, and to sow discord among them. When we harbor anger in our heart, we do the devil's work for him. Our forgiveness to others is patterned after the forgiveness of Jesus towards us. When we think of the amazing way God forgives us, it is shameful for us to withhold forgiveness from those who have wronged us.

Stealing in the body of Christ is about so much more than just the materialistic things that can be attained. Many can be found stealing other people's joy, self esteem, and vision. However when we have put on the new man, the new man does not steal. Instead he does everything he can to add to not take from the body of Christ. This includes knowing how to watch his tongue, speaking only what is good necessary for edification, desiring to impart grace to all who hear him. This does not only apply to vulgar language or cussing, it also applies to gossip, slander and belittling language meant to put people down.

Lastly, the new man does all that he can not to grieve the Holy Spirit. The new man thinks of more than materialistic gain; He looks to holiness and exalts Jesus at every opportunity he can. The new man's prayer life is of monumental importance and his study of the Bible takes precedent over engaging in folly. The new man does not spend more time on worldly things than he does with God. In this way he feeds his inner spirit and does not grieve the Spirit.

Even after reading everything so far. You still may be wondering how any of this applies to what the real church should look like. My response is the real church should be full of likeminded people, those who are willing to say not my will be done but thy will be done; those who meet together to share with one another the true reality of Christ in their lives. What has He taught you and how have you changed? This is the real church: those who are being conformed to the image of Christ, sharing their experiences with one another, encouraging and supporting one another as they go.

Very simply put Colossians 2:5-7 tells us what God intended and what the Scriptures describe: believers standing together, drawing strength from one another determined to live with Him and be like Him and having the very foundation of their lives firmly established on the things He is teaching them and being thankful for His participation in their lives. Now that is the real church and not religion.

Meet Cheryl Lacey Donovan

Cheryl draws on her experience and passion as an educator to motivate and encourage others to live their lives on purpose. She is particularly passionate about helping others create the lives they deserve and desire. Articulate and compassionate, Cheryl is a speaker with a gift for teaching. She says, "My desire is to help people see the world from God's perspective, and to move them to do something about what they see." Cheryl has spent a lifetime acquiring experience around educating and advising others on living a more meaningful life. After more than 20 years of educating and advising allied health care professionals Cheryl followed her passion for bringing out the best in other people by choosing to be more involved in the vision and direction their lives were taking. This culminated in the launch of Worth More than Rubies a division or Cheryl Lacey Donovan International. Since then Cheryl has spoken to hundreds of groups across the country and written articles as well as Bible study curricula. Cheryl is uniquely positioned to impact the lives of individuals she comes in contact with for long term success with her message of faith and powerful vision of bringing purpose into the people equation to promote happier, healthier more meaningful life experiences. Cheryl presents a powerful message with a conversational style that's just like sitting around chatting with one of your sisters - one who is filled with pearls of wisdom and whose heart is filled with giving. Some of us long for that kind of sister or friend who will just sit you down, tell you the truth about life, share her experiences, and then give you access to a greater more meaningful purpose in life. You will want to sip a warm cup of your favorite drink, bring a note pad and enjoy a candid and educational presentation with Cheryl Lacey Donovan.

www.ingramcontent.com/pod-product-compliance
Lightning Source LLC
Chambersburg PA
CBHW051827090426

42736CB00011B/1680